Too Little Too Late

How the world is about to end

(if we don't do something about it I mean)

By Niall Brennan

Contents

5: I don't trust us
- Danger in dangerous hands
- War, nuclear and otherwise
- Population growth
- Western social morass

6: And just all the other normal stuff.
- Solar flares
- Asteroids
- Volcanoes
- Cosmic outbursts
- The Fermi Paradox

7: What needs to be done
- Get elected
- Tyrants, monsters and destroyers of Earth
- Fight for our survival
- Run for election
- Get elected (simple, right?)

8: References. For you. Not for me. Where to go next, in other words.

Bibliography online.

Introduction and overview

I will describe the future of this world exactly as it is going to unfold. I know this is hubris, and I agree it is nearly impossible. Nevertheless, the main point of this book is that we have set in motion a very large number of circumstances which seem likely to destroy the world we live in, or impact our lives irreversibly and I doubt we have the capacity to outrun them all. In fact, I worry that we're about to be overtaken much sooner than we think, as the evidence herein should help you conclude. Though I will describe a great many ways the world is in danger, the human capacity to overcome adversity is immense. I don't want to dampen anyone's enthusiasm for the enormous effort that must be made, but the time to act is now. I fear we have reached the very brink.

It's now or never. Even if it is too late to completely stop any of the coming disasters, we have no real choice other than damage-limitation, while we take a Hail-Mary punt on some hopeful dreams about the future of human society and technology. We desperately need change, and I fear the changes needed will only be recognised when it's far too late. How many species must become extinct before we truly realise we are witnessing an apocalyptic event? I will try to propose some sensible solutions after I've scared you enough about the future. But, ultimately, you will not like the message I will espouse; it is already too late to be nice. The time for drastic and potentially evil things is upon us.

With an optimistic mind-set you could say we have already reached a grand realisation and will convince a massive change in our collective outlook, in time, and with the good fortune to find solutions too. With an objective consideration of the evidence however, you could easily conclude we have passed the point of no return already or the creeping deadlines will pass us soon because it seems we will never have the unity of will or technological capability to sustain ourselves and we have absolutely no intention of limiting our growth.

I don't wish to inflict our younger generation with further anxiety and resentment but it is far beyond time for a complete reconsideration of the nature of our relationship with our environment. It's not just about global warming; it's about our rampant growth, consumption, technological advancement, and pollution, coupled with a totally untethered *raison d'etre;* we have no meaning, no purpose. We have fostered a greedy, malicious morality of expansion and profit that no god would even bother to drown, so certain is its doom; why would He send a flood for us when we're making one ourselves? I beg you, let me make you aware in this book of how many ways we are about to face a radical change in our environment and lifestyles that seem to constitute some dystopian apocalypse, according to a wide range of authoritative sources. Any one source can only ring the alarm bell for its own set of interests. The bigger picture is dreadful.

We are all broadly aware that there is growing noise about a wide-range of environmental issues, and that it's being acknowledged as never before, but the urgency of the situation hasn't sunk into the zeitgeist yet. The simplest illustration is that we are now almost universally recognising that sea-rise is inexorable. If we were to cease all technological activity globally tomorrow and turn off everything, the ice would continue to melt for hundreds of years from all the pollution we've already done. Our most progressive response to this as a world united is to hope to wean us off carbon in time to limit the acceleration. That's a worthy fight for us, but the real implications of what we younger generations will inevitably witness therefore are terrifying. Too many cities for us to sensibly defend are going to sink into the sea. Whole countries. And people still build seafront properties! Winning in this situation is to perhaps not have to watch too many cities collapse in our lifetimes. Losing in this situation is only slightly worse, because our grandchildren will have to watch anyway in the best case scenario.

I will go on to explore this in more detail, but the real crux of the example I've just very briefly touched upon is that it's not a simple and untangled issue. There are more problems than you are aware of, mounting more quickly than you can imagine. It is most assuredly beyond our individual scope to understand the grand scale of our population growth in the last century, combined with our growth in material wealth, globally. It is an unfathomably enormous change that has been little noted. We are very truly hypnotised by our collective memory of how unchangeable and dependable the world was just a short time ago. So much so that we think **we** haven't really changed much and that life goes on as it did before. But it doesn't, we have dramatically, and the living world isn't at all what it once was; it is diminishing rapidly.

Our incredible transformation has changed the whole world, and for us all the better, but not for the rest. We must digest the truth that we are a plague upon this earth, as Sir David Attenborough so eloquently put it. It is not a single issue of global warming. It is a wild toxic myriad of dangers all being compounded by our activities, by our poor stewardship and by our reckless growth. The problem is us. The only solution must be us. No superheroes are coming to rescue us. The great beard in the sky will not save us. We can only do it ourselves. And what needs to be done is simply grim, not hopeful. Too many on the green side want to paint the future in rainbows. The truth is harder.

Even if in some of the cases I explore in this book it's already too late and in others I doubt we will avoid the tipping points, we must endeavour to limit the damage. We must. With whatever consequences that entails. We must change the relationship of humanity and Earth. We must essentially transcend nature. In order to undertake such a ridiculous quest, we must have a ridiculously good reason. To this end, I want to collate a series of irrefutable growing dangers and add them up for you in a way that makes you realise it is not enough to think about alterations to our individual behaviour in order to address various individual issues. There are at least 25 quite different man-made catastrophes unfolding that require a holistic solution, at least that's how many my sanity could bear to address in writing this book. We must address the whole problem.

This is about our moral compass as stewards of life. We have come to lack any sense of the profundity of our position as human beings. We seem to be the only species we can see anywhere capable of thinking like we do, so we have a responsibility to think hard. We are the only thing capable of reading and writing, so it too is a profound duty. Any beast can look at a screen, but nothing can read what is here like you. The compounding effects of so many looming catastrophes on a global scale, which I'm about to describe in this book, should make you realise that we need to address all of these issues together, on the whole, and that includes our most fundamental values and beliefs. We need a drastic overhaul of everything, from here to there to everywhere. We need a new understanding. A new covenant.

I don't offer one, certainly nothing palatable to normal people, though I offer what I think of as the 'sensible' options we will have to face. I would love to write the new scripture that sets the world alight, but this is not it. This is a prophecy of doom. I intend to take the 'I-told-you-so' high-ground. I also want to change the world, as I'm sure you do too, given you're reading this. The end is nigh, unless our entire species demonstrates its collective intelligence and cooperation on a scale never seen before. What we require and seemingly expect according to current political rhetoric is absolute global alignment between 198+ nations and 7.747

billion people (2/12/19). There is a lot of evidence to suggest it will not be achieved.

Obviously I hope it could be done. But then again, I hope China is invaded for the atrocities they are currently committing against their Muslim minorities; The Uighur people are being 'cleansed'. I would not cooperate with China even if they did the 'right' thing. I've lived there, and know their system is absolutely corrupt. So, although certain solutions, or hopes for solutions, are mooted, my position is that these things are worthless without a unity of purpose that pervades the entire species. This seems unlikely to be achieved in my lifetime. But disaster in my lifetime seems overwhelmingly likely, which I will of course explain. So what of it? Are we to sit and watch our children starve and choke and have their houses washed away? I won't. I will fight.

However strongly I feel and empathise with the intolerable suffering of people around the world, saving people from suffering is not what this is about. The problem is more systemic than geopolitics. It is only a matter of the macro-economics of sustainability and survival. Give me the magic wand and I would sweep away the enduring indignity that seems to come with the grinding progress of development, but I couldn't halt the development itself without myself committing atrocious grievance. I couldn't enforce an equality of resource sharing, without dissolving a lot of people's comfort and dignity. People deserve to have an equal share of comfort and dignity, don't they? And yet we seem bound for disaster if we were to imagine an equality of consumption for all.

If every adult had a car, we'd be goosed. If every adult got a steak per week, we'd starve. I have done a lot of research into discussions about feeding our burgeoning population, quickly heading to 8 billion, but they all seem like science fiction. I'll discuss this further inside. I love it, but at the same time, I'm very afraid. I hope we can do it, but I doubt it.

Sustainably? Why ever would you think so? We face a fundamental problem. Not just an environmental or political or financial problem; a fundamental problem. And therefore our fundamentals are still wrong. We have evolved massively in the last century and it has been a glorious time of love and wellbeing in the 'great peace' of Europe, but it is not the end-state of a sustainable civilisation. Not yet. I fear we are a generation ahead of our time; dreaming of peace while the biggest war of them all looms.

As I am writing this book, a new decade begins and it seems to me it will be the decade of mounting fear of environmental catastrophe. It will be the biggest thing talked about everywhere. Not only will I outline a number of reasons why you should be scared, as I am, about the future of our species, but I will also write about some of the ways in which I think we can remedy our collective ideological disillusionment that lead us to further fear. It seems politics has become an exclusive category all of its own in which all the other aspects of human existence have been estranged from the conversation. The only real hope has to be political, one way or another. Please suffer this quick dose.

Politics has become a vehicle for policy changes in the civil service and a question of balancing expenditure with revenue. It no longer seems 'politick' to use politics for ideology. We no longer want leaders who tell us how we should live our lives and what our goals and purposes should be and it is deeply flawed to omit anything from political thinking. All aspects of human experience fall under the remit of political aspiration! It is a sign of our collective disillusionment that some people can refuse to talk about serious things but still expect to have their opinions taken seriously, and way of life preserved. If you have anything serious to say, then you are politicking! We are political creatures! The only solution to our collective problems that can be achieved is through political action. Drastic as needs be. And hard dissent has been a political staple of our species;

potentially the last tool we have to awaken and revitalise our civilisation.

What we really need is some messianic figure, or some brilliant manifesto that sets the world on fire and unites the entire species in some semi-divine purpose or political revolution. You will probably be more optimistic than me in thinking that leaders are arising, and consensus is growing, but I urgently need to dispel the notion that people are going to change effectively enough and quickly enough to save the world in a happy and peaceful way without a serious change in attitudes. For one thing, the reason this prophecy of doom or the needed manifesto of unity will not work is that not enough people are simply keeping up to date with scientific discoveries, understandings and consensus. This is obviously because a lot of scientific consensus currently contradicts a great deal of our previously strongly held positions, such as in understanding the origin of the universe or the evolution of life.

How can we possibly hope to achieve anything when the intelligentsia and academia of our society have been side-lined in favour of vacuous celebrity culture? Or when thoroughly ratified scientific principles are disbelieved like evolution? If some silly god were to whisper the newest gospel into the ears of the latest charlatan claiming to be a 'prophet', it would go no further than that, as the likelihood is that very few people would read it. The most widely-read books on earth right now could not be called anything other than 'widely-unread' if one were to be objective about any one readership around the world. Despite education pushing back fundamental illiteracy in recent years, it has done nothing to stem the rising tide of hedonism, individualism and tolerated ignorance that come with great numbers.

I do not think there is much hope left, but I cling desperately to what remains. There must still be time to do SOMETHING. The time may soon come when those who are convinced will need to adopt almost-militant positions in order to spread the message any further. If there isn't a huge swing to green and highly-progressive politics in the next decade, there won't be the action needed to escape the ten-year deadline of carbon emissions. We need many candidates to present themselves immediately, in all democracies. If we don't take decisive action ten minutes ago, we will not save the species we share this earth with. We are living in the worst extinction event the earth has ever known; worse than any asteroid or volcano, it bears reminding. If we don't dedicate a sizeable proportion of all budgets and 'manpower hours' to the cause of environmental clean-up, we will be brought to complete collapse forthwith.

I would go to any lengths and support any lunatic whose goal would be to simply shut down the coal and turf furnaces. I see ANY action, no matter how inflammatory or damaging, justifiable means to this end. We must enlist the masses by any means necessary. We must convince enough people to take matters into their own hands that changes will be brought about no matter the attitude of the rest. The rest of you can get on side or get out of the way. You will sit in the dark until other electricity is made, because some of us will do whatever it takes to close down the electricity generation that is ruining the world. We must fight for this. It's too late for phasing, slow transition, and oil companies tricking us into the latest carbon-saving gadget that actually requires gas or coal or hydrogen (derived from gas) that will come in twenty years, with the gap bridged with accelerated burning of coal and turf! It's too little. Hopefully though, it's not too late, though barely. We have to move now to change everything about our way of life and it will hurt a lot of people a great deal. It might be too late to stop everything, but we must try.

We need to get angry and only with the hope of limiting the apocalypse, not stopping it. Imagine how angry you'll be if we do pass some point of no return one day and we might have actually stopped it if someone had said this 30 years ago… In fact, we've known for much longer than that. It's almost the point of no return today. We are on the brink of a collapse, and it is not the slow decay for our grandchildren and beyond that we feared previously; it is an immediate and intolerable threat to anyone young enough to not be an ignoramus about the world and our place in it. I am furious with our forebears for leaving us this ugly reality, but I am equally furious that my generation is not eating each other alive in their efforts to fix it. In short; I think we might soon be fucked. So let's fight for our survival.

It may seem grim, but how grim simply depends on how much faith you have in humanity. And we are one hell of a magical species upon this tiny mote in god's eye.

So before we begin; it is always the case that someone else can say it better, so here are three perfectly succinct quotes to digest:

"It is unrealistic to think that the future of humanity can be achieved only on the basis of prayer; what we need is to take action" The immortal Dalai Lama

"The future of humanity is going to bifurcate in two directions: either it's going to become multiplanetary or it's going to remained confined to one planet and eventually there's going to be an extinction event" The possibly immortal Elon Musk

"I will never apologise for saying that the future of humanity and the future of the world is going to be defined by what we have in common as opposed to those things that separate us and ultimately lead us into conflict" The hopefully immortal Barack Obama

1: The oceans

The oceans are the very cradle of life itself. All life started in the oceans, as far as we can tell, from the very simple to the very complex; everything's ancestors. It is well-known and roundly criticised that even today the oceans are both our larder and our sewer. It is well-known that overfishing and dumping are causing damage to the ocean environment on a level unseen anywhere on land. The one thing that I don't think is well-known, or at least well-appreciated, is how crucial the oceans are for life on land. We think of the jungles as the lungs of the world, and yet they produce only part of the oxygen we enjoy. The Phytoplankton of the oceans are much more important.

We think of biodiversity in terms of jungles and mountains and deserts and islands, but in reality, there is more diversity in a healthy coral reef than in a continental jungle. We do not seem to understand that a sterile ocean inexorably means a sterile planet. We could burn the jungles to the ground and still survive if the ocean biome remained healthy (well maybe not). But if the oceans were badly affected, the jungles would collapse alongside. Water is life. All life on earth lives in symbiosis; all life is connected through our literal sharing of water. How many living things has the water that's in you now passed through? A bloody mind-boggling number. Maybe the water thinks it's alive too.

I think most people (at least those people who are paying attention) know and understand that there are a number of issues that are very concerning to environmentalists around the world at the moment with regards to the oceans, and other bodies of water. A large number of people, with the help of the media, are aware of the plastic crisis, but awareness is not the same as appreciation and understanding. Many people do appreciate that most coastal cities are still pouring raw, untreated sewage into the ocean, but people still seem to think this just means natural excrement and think it enriches the ocean with food particles. It's so much terribly more than that. It's also all the substances washed off our streets and directed down drains. It's every chemical known to humanity, all the time and all at once, as well as all our terrible waste.

Many people know that fishing has changed and that people talk about 'overfishing'. First of all, we are far beyond eating more farmed fish than caught. This is to satiate demand, not because of responsible management of supply. What I think people fail to realise is that 'fishing' practices now are no longer really 'fishing'; they are industrialised purposeful eradication of populations. 'Fishing' sounds like you pick one creature out of a shoal. What we have now is the absolute and complete destruction of any shoals that form anywhere. Everyone seems to be aware of these issues, but the gravity of the situation seems to be missed. In a nutshell; there are grave problems with the oceans, and the most likely cause of global apocalyptic catastrophe will be there, not in the ice-caps or the jungles or the bushfires, and there is imminent danger.

Let's start with plastic. Thanks to Newscorp (sky, sun, fox, etc.) we are more widely aware than ever that there is a crisis in the ocean with plastic. (Thanks, surprisingly, empire of Murdoch; you know it's bad when giant evil corporations are afraid.) However, the very way in which this debate is framed is incredibly flawed. Proactive measures to prevent plastic going into the oceans completely miss the point, although still necessary. It's far too late to start thinking about how you limit the amount of plastic going into the oceans; that time was over 70 years ago. What we actually need now is some (magical) way of removing the plastic we've already put there. Further than that, the issue isn't so much to do with the simplistic problem of fish and birds eating the plastic; it's got much more to do with the very nature of plastic itself. Did you know that most of the chemicals and materials that we have developed in the last century are untested in terms of their long-term effects on our health or environment? Have you ever considered if wrapping your sandwiches in cellophane is advisable? Do you have any idea how many dangerous and destructive chemicals and processes go into making all the artificial products the world has come to depend on?

It is absolutely bloody mind-bendingly ludicrous. Our juvenile tampering with materials we know little about is comparable to the stealing of fire by Prometheus. We have unlocked a multitude of secrets and recipes from nature, but we haven't given a thought to whether we should. The perfect example of this comes from the first few decades of plastic production. Plastic has only been around for a little over a hundred years. The first ever plastic, and the plastic that spread around the world like wildfire after the war, was a substance known as 'bakelite' or polyoxybenzylmethylenglycolanhydride, a name to strike fear into your heart. Bakelite is unimaginably dangerous and it represents a Pandora's box that we opened, whose lid we shall never ever close again. The problem with Bakelite is that a few years after it first started to be widely incorporated into manufacture in a newly accelerated consumerist society, the substance was discovered to be decaying in ways we never expected. Currently about 8 million tonnes of plastic reach the oceans each year and there are already more than 150 million tonnes out there, of which a few million are Bakelite.

If you have a plastic object in your house from the forties and fifties, like a doll your grandmother had, you will recognise that this type of plastic degraded in an unpredictable way, as its colour changes over time. When the polymer chains in this plastic break down, a myriad of extremely toxic and carcinogenic chemicals are released. You will notice with certain plastics and elastics that they turn into a jelly over time and almost liquefy; this is the breakdown of their chemistry. Wherever you see plastic discolour or decay through exposure to the elements, you can be sure that the chemical reactions taking place are poorly understood and the effects on our health in the long-term are unknown. The real problem with Bakelite was that it is biodegradable. We stopped using Bakelite pretty rapidly when we discovered just how noxious it was, but decades of its waste was poured into the oceans first. It naturally decays and releases petro-chemical toxins and this process is catalysed by exposure to sunlight and salt water.

The other side of the plastic problem is the newer 'non-biodegradable' plastic. Firstly, of course they do degrade, but at a very slow rate chemically. However, that slow rate of chemical degradation is countered by the relatively quick rate of physical degradation. Large amounts of the plastic in the ocean come from torn and broken plastic equipment such as fishing ropes, lines and nets. These pieces get broken down further by being torn at by rotors and sea-creatures and break down into tiny little pieces that are simply impossible to remove, so small as to be nearly invisible and these tiny pieces are so much more dangerous to sea life than large pieces of trash. For one thing creatures cannot and do not discern the difference between these tiny flecks and plankton, so they slowly accumulate indigestible materials that climb the food chain and do grave damage to the soft tissues and organs of their bodies.

The other issue with the tiny particles is how widely dispersed they can become in a very short period of time. If you drop a bucket into any ocean or sea anywhere in the world, you will find lots and lots of little bits of plastic; an unbelievable amount; it has gotten at least twice as bad as the last time you looked. This problem cannot be overstated and is widely underestimated. It is not even nearly just confined to the gyres. The oceans are literally choking on plastic. The accumulation of so many little molecules also has a detrimental effect on photosynthesising plankton as they block out light and compete for space. Those little molecules are now being incorporated into the flesh of the sea-creatures we eat, causing infections and cancers that seriously endanger species we depend on. And all of this is without considering the big headlines of plastic contamination like the garbage gyre in the pacific, or to consider how big and exotic creatures are affected. That continent sized garbage pile is easily our ugliest sin and we're killing all sorts of bigger animals with it. One of the worst examples is the death of the birds of Midway; one of the most isolated places on earth, their stomachs filled with bottle caps and polystyrene. It is a tragedy too hard to contemplate.

While modern plastics are hardier and less degradable than their forebears, they are not completely so. They do break down chemically over time, although it is a very long time. They have a very superficial benefit of not immediately toxifying the whole world, but it is such a gross insult to our children and grandchildren. We banned the use of a substance in our own lifetime that would have had grave health effects, but we doubled down on the production of material that would be equally harmful in a couple of hundred years, especially when exposed to harsh conditions such as those in the oceans or in our landfills. 'Double' in this 'double-down' context is orders of magnitude too small a word. But you're picking up what I'm laying down by this point, I'd imagine.

We also need to consider the processes that go into making these more durable plastic polymers. Plastic is the cheapest bi-product of the petro-chemical industry, but it is a petro-chemical process. Unlike some other industrial productions these days that result in huge pools of poisonous toxins that slowly seep into the groundwater, plastic production cannot let its by-products and catalysers coalesce in collection pools, with the chemicals released being so wildly toxic that they could never hope to be contained. Instead these bi-products are fed back into the process and recycled to a large degree, but not completely. Plastic production off-gases toxins that would have otherwise caused the plastics to decay as Bakelite did. Instead of letting people take home products which will decay into carcinogens in their houses, we pump it into the air and let a future generation pay for the cost. And please don't talk to me about plant-based plastic production. Will ye get real? We can't burn down the forests fast enough just to produce food. We'll look at that problem in more detail elsewhere.

In this book I don't necessarily want to waste your time telling you things that should be widely known; that you SHOULD know already if you were paying attention at all. But I expect you will not know about the acidification of the oceans. Please google the acidification of the oceans. I was completely unaware of this from mass media. Needless to say, it's really very bad. Despite the fact that more and more fresh water is entering the water cycle and should in theory be diluting the ocean of its harmful chemicals somewhat, we observe on the contrary that concentrations of a wide number of toxic chemicals are increasing throughout the ocean. At an even higher rate than we can account for, in fact. And the PH level of the ocean is changing fast.

This must largely be attributed to the increased levels of carbon in the air, which the ocean absorbs about 40% of, and converts to carbonic acid. This is one of wildly many causes. And I could not overstate how bad it is for the PH levels of our oceans to change. It literally causes almost everything to die horrifically. Almost nothing will survive this if it continues for another hundred years. The oceans will be completely sterile. This could mostly be said to be a 'natural' result or side-effect of our non-ocean pollution; the carbon footprint crisis, and this is where attention is starting to get directed, but there are other causes too. They come from a wide range of really bad contaminations of our waterways and water tables and seas for so long and in so many ways. We cannot look at every leak and spill in history, but just for one quick universal example; consider batteries.

Battery production uses about 6 million tons of lead-acid each year, amongst a bunch of other toxic stuff. Up until recently almost all of this went to landfill and reached our water table. Since the popularisation of lead recycling (for economic reasons, not environmental ones), the problem of released toxins has in fact increased. This is because the processes for recovering the lead are haphazard and poorly governed. I point this example out as the most widespread impact that each of us as individuals contribute to this problem, but this is only one among many. When you google that aforesaid 'ocean acidification', you will find page after page of information about how carbon is affecting the ocean, but you will have to dig diligently to find the rest.

I will cover some of these in relation to other catastrophes too. However, for your quick edification, here is a list of some of the groups of causes of the acidification:
- fertilisers entering the water table,
-the effects of rare-earth mining on the water table as well as other mining and drilling practices such as 'fracking',
-the reduced capacity of the ocean to remove acid due to damaging fishing practices that scrape off essential filter feeders and carbon sinks,
-the use of harsh chemicals throughout the world for cleaning and washing with the proliferation of non-biological washing products, which is equally harmful no matter where you are,
-the dramatically increased number of dead and decaying creatures in the ocean as a result of fishing by-kill. These are just a few of the things. Don't google them all at once or you will become violently angry.

Quite aside from all the horrifying ways in which acidification is being accelerated as we speak, there are also **other** contamination issues that are widely acknowledged as being problematic for future generations. Consider mercury. A tiny quantity of mercury has extremely negative effects on all biological creatures, and so far we've pumped somewhere between 40 and 80 thousand metric tonnes of this into the oceans. This material, when ingested, never leaves the system of a creature, and accumulates in higher and higher quantities as you climb the food chain. Most of this mercury is within a couple of miles of our shores as this substance doesn't dilute as well as other chemicals we release.

Quite a lot of our sea-life lives within a short distance from shore. Have you ever eaten oysters, mussels, prawns or scallops? Where do you think they live? Have you ever considered where and how they feed? We eat the very creatures who are most likely to be absorbing mercury. Now the mercury issue isn't as apocalyptic as most of the issues I am going to discuss here, but it is a wonderful illustration of how our awareness of environmental issues isn't matched by sensible actions. If you continue to eat the bottom-feeders of our toxic sewer, then you are foolish, but you're in good company as most of the population does the same, even I until just now.

We can easily see and understand these big-ticket issues affecting the oceans, though we seem to be grossly reticent in adjusting our lifestyles to fit the truths we understand. However, there a number of other huge contaminations that are not widely acknowledged, but have equally devastating effects. We know that the vast majority of people on earth live in coastal towns and cities. We know that a growing number of these cities and towns are completely surfaced in concrete, tarmac and asphalt. We know that these towns and cities are bursting with cars and vehicles. We know that through wear and tear, as well as through exhaust fumes, chemicals accumulate on our roads and streets and in the dust we breathe. Cities are well-drained and especially well-drained where better road infrastructure is in place.

In short, the more accommodating to cars and trucks a place becomes, the quicker and more efficiently the waste products of these vehicles is washed into the sea. One of the best places to find rare and noxious minerals is in the catalytic converters of our cars, and subsequently in the dust that accumulates on the sides of roads. Almost every chemical known to man is washed into the sea along with all our conventional sewage in this way. We cannot predict the effects of such widespread disregard for the environment, and we cannot dream of doing anything about it. How can you prevent dust from washing into the sea? We must instead limit it. Grim. We must limit the development of roads and sewers no matter what we intend to put on or in them. This will be grossly unfair on the poorest nations, who will need help.

The contamination of our oceans with man-made chemicals has exploded in the last century to a degree that you can't possible comprehend. We look at all the benefits we have received in the last century and take them for granted, but in fact they are all brand new, and almost all temporary. We cannot continue to drive diesel and petrol cars for very much longer and they've only been around a couple of generations, but already we are so dependent on them that we can barely imagine the world without them. We do not appreciate just how much human activity has changed. A hundred years ago in most cities on earth, most of what washed off them into the sea was of a natural biological nature and people travelled by foot or horse. There were of course contaminations earlier in the industrial revolution, but these went from being the responsibility of a few elite consumers, to being the widespread norm for any aspiring populace. Everyone wants to use the chemicals and products and machines that have made our lives so easy.

When sewers were built in the West, the vast majority of what went into them was what is meant to go into them. Now every sewerage system on earth suffers from the same problems as we do in big western cities. The amount of wet-wipes, diapers, ear-buds and household chemicals being dumped this way is astronomical. That is quite aside from all the many cities where there is no sewerage at all. The sea is our sewer, and only a few rich western countries have slightly improved that position. Even in the best cities, where sewage is processed before release, there is still the problem of what to do with all the liquid once the 'solid' waste is recycled. We treat chemical contamination with chemicals. We simply cannot limit our reckless dumping of chemicals into the sea without radically limiting our own creature-comforts and rampant consumption. Do you want to tell the poor people who wash their clothes directly in the Ganges river that they shouldn't use chemical soap that will keep their children alive while doing so? Ridiculous. We must instead improve their lot.

The next thing to talk about is the oil. A few years ago, when BP had their big oil-spill in the Gulf of Mexico, the news swept through the world immediately. People got very upset. The remonstrations were decried from on high. It was a disaster. It was catastrophic for life in the region. The damage very quickly spread from the sea to the land through the marshlands of southern USA. However, this one spillage is only one drop in the gigantic bucket of oil contamination the world's oceans have suffered. This spill barely registers as 'large' in the records. Since the beginning of off-shore oil production, there have been at least 239 medium-to-large recorded spills from wells, releasing untold millions of gallons of unprocessed oil directly into the oceans.

These large spills tend to be widely acknowledged and publicised, but bizarrely, the much bigger issue of oil-tankers seems to be widely ignored. Most oil produced on earth is transported across the sea in gigantic tankers. Some oil and gas is also transported through pipelines. The amount of spillage caused by these sources is outrageous. Since 1970, there have been more than 4.9 million litres of oil lost to the sea just from reported tanker spills, and who knows before then. If you add up all the estimated oil lost from wells, 'natural' seeps, leaking pipelines and lost vehicles you end up with ridiculous numbers. We have lost billions of barrels; billions and billions of litres; stupendous amounts. In the first hundred and fifty years we consumed a trillion barrels of oil and we've consumed another trillion in the last thirty. A trillion more and it's gone. Of that billions have been lost. Suffice it to say, we are quickly killing the oceans with oil. It's in a race with plastic.

But this is, once again, an issue that many of us SHOULD be aware of. There are quite ingenious people working on solutions for cleaning up some of the worst effects of these spills. The companies themselves use harsh chemical substances to try to neutralise and break up the oils… oh wait… and giant plastic booms and nets are deployed to try to contain the spread of this oil... ah wait… These efforts only manage to contain a very small part of the contamination, so this issue alone is catastrophic and unsustainable anyway. That being said, our off-shore production continues to increase(!), and the number of tankers continues to increase. We are increasingly dependent on oil despite our wide acknowledgement that we need to stop using it.

It cannot be stressed enough how silly and indefensible our continued attitude towards oil is. Even if you don't buy into the FACT that it is causing global warming, and contaminating the lands and seas where it is produced, you must surely accept that it is a finite resource. We will one day run out of oil, so our continued increase(!) in its production and our increasing dependency on it is astoundingly stupid. I say 'increase with a (!)', because although we continue to look for and exploit new sources of oil and gas, and burn more than ever, our ability to maintain production levels in the face of rampant consumption is failing. Peak oil production was more than ten years ago. We are now on the downward slope of production rates, as wells dry up and reserves are being tapped. We are absolutely guaranteed to see oil run out this century, even if we conserve. More on this in the Resources section.

This is quite apocalyptic on its own, but let me tell you about a scary and widely unknown danger that is about to become a massive problem. The problem I'm about to describe is the 'dirty oil in sunken ships' problem. In the early days of oil production, oil was very inefficiently used, as processes were still being developed. Nowadays we use a large number of chemical processes to separate out all the constituent parts of oil for their various industrial applications. This was not always the case and many of the earliest ships and vehicles used a product called 'dirty oil'. Dirty oil is a deeply inefficient and noxious substance, but in the early days of its use was a miraculous source of seemingly 'free' energy. Thousands of ships were merrily loaded with it and sent on their way. The introduction of this ridiculously toxic substance to the world unfortunately coincided with the two most vicious wars ever fought, in which a very large number of ships were sunk. It is estimated that there are over 8000 sunken ships lying at the bottom of our oceans from world war 2 alone and altogether with other ships containing anywhere between 500 million litres and 4.5 billion litres of oil. These ships have languished under enormous pressure for a lifetime, and are just about ready to release their contents.

You will notice that ALL the tanker spills in history add up to somewhere in the middle of that estimate. If you take into account the oxidisation rate of iron and how long it takes for sunken ships to disintegrate, our best estimate is that in the next 20 +/- years, more oil will spill from these sunken wrecks than all the known oil-containing ships that have been wrecked in the past 70 years. The upper end of the estimate for how much oil is inevitably about to spill is more than all the known man-made oil spills in history combined.

That is a crazy number, and impossible to wrap you head around, but please take a moment to think about what this means for future generations. We DO NOT have the ability or technology to prevent these ships from rusting through, or extracting the oil before it is released into the ocean.

Inevitably, inexorably and inescapably, we will live to see oil contamination in the oceans and on our coasts on a scale never seen before. This is one of those issues where I can't see a way out, and I can't imagine a way to even limit the damage it will cause. And the worst thing about all of this is, it continues. We continue to send ships full of oil out onto the water. We still run pipes that can only last a limited amount of time before they spring a leak. We still seek out new wells to be tapped, and build new offshore platforms. This is just crazy! How can this be the case? How can we so knowingly sprint towards our own destruction? I would rather fight, die and cause suffering than let this continue in my name. It's time to turn the lights off.

And I do mean it when I say we are heading for our own destruction, from the sea. On average, our per capita consumption of those who eat seafood is 20kg per year. There are at least 155 million tonnes of seafood extracted from the oceans each year. This is completely and unacceptably unsustainable. 90% of all fish have been wiped out in the last 50 years. I reckon there are less than ten years left in our global fishing industry. Tuna, once unimaginably abundant, has been almost eradicated from the earth in a lifetime, and its last remnants are being hunted relentlessly, with factory ships ploughing the waters from the arctic to the Antarctic. Cod and Trout are on the brink of extinction. Anchovies' and sardines' official status is 'not extinct', but heading that way rapidly. I can't sufficiently express just how destructive fishing practices have become in the last couple of centuries. When the European colonists arrived in the gulf of St. Lawrence in Canada, the progress of ships was slowed, such was the volume of fish passing beneath. You could barely stick an oar in the water without catching some fish. Now you can starve there with a fishing rod in your hand. Salmon have been pushed from most of the rivers beneath the arctic circle, and is now either fished from its remaining strongholds or farmed.

The barbarism of our fishing practices would be astounding to anyone outside of the industry. Where most of our seafood is sourced in such an appalling and obviously unsustainable way, it is actually the traditional fishermen that are highlighting the utter stupidity of the current industry. They're being put out of business globally; being put out of sustenance in fact. There are gigantic factory ships out there on the ocean with nets the size of counties, with hundreds of people working on board in despicable conditions returning to shore only occasionally to sell the product of their destruction. In recent years some of these ships were found to be operating modern day slavery rings.

You show up at a port in one of the poorest cities on earth, sign a few hundred workers to come on board for a few years and then sail away into the sunset. There was a ship found only a few years ago, where the crew had been trapped on board for 3 years, working for payment in fish. Each day they would work 18 hour shifts in an airless, stinking fish-hold in 40-45-degree heat, 7 days a week, for no money; walk the plank if you've got a problem. And this shockingly sad human drama is not even close to the problem I have with this operation. You may well be appalled with this, as I am, but this isn't the unsustainable part. However horrific our treatment of other humans may be, it is unlikely to cause an apocalyptic catastrophe. And by the way, it is our consumption of those products that is to blame, not the desperate producers.

The unsustainable part is how the fishing is actually done. You'll be aware of course that nets on these super-trawlers are ridiculously large and strong. You will probably also know that there are regulations governing how big the gaps in the mesh are in order to limit the by-kill or bycatch. The quota system and other regulations designed to prevent the eradication of fish stocks do not take into account the rampant growth in the fishing industry, nor the simple nature of sea-life sustainability. These super trawlers can stay at sea longer and are pimped out with tech, and their nets are so large and durable that no shoal escapes their attention.

They are also catching everything else that is preying on that shoal, as well as all the other creatures that happen to be swimming by AS WELL AS the fact that these giant nets scrape the seabed clean. The scraping of the seabed is one of the most horrible effects of these giant nets. Plant-life in relatively shallow seas such as reeds, as well as various corrals, sponges and bottom-feeders are destroyed in this process at an alarming and unsustainable rate. The eradication of this part of the ecosystem is problematic for the seas' ability to cleanse itself of the other contaminants and effects previously mentioned. The disturbance of the silt and mud of the sea-floor is utterly disgusting when you consider what we have dumped there over the past century too. We are rapidly causing the desertification of the ocean floor.

In every significant catch of tuna, there are likely to be dolphins and porpoises also trapped. In recent years the extremely dubious self-reported bycatch figures show a huge reduction; up to 99%, of the number of creatures incidentally killed when particular species are targeted. This can only mean one of two things; either the numbers of these creatures have reached such low levels as to be negligible, or much more likely, the trawlers have learned to not report by-kill. It is fairly obvious that companies who are willing to employ slaves are not going to pay much attention to quotas and regulations around reporting bycatch. If they are reporting the truth, expect an almost immediate collapse. They obviously just abuse the system.

I think the most glaring evidence of this abuse is in the figures being reported, even by the industry itself, never mind the many appalled observers. It is simply impossible for there to have been a 99% reduction in bycatch while fish hauls have increased by 50% in twenty years. How has the quota system allowed such growth in the first place? It is ridiculous that we are expected to believe the fishing industry has improved its practices, when all evidence not supplied by the industry seems to suggest they are completely out of control and essentially operating in total contempt of the law; of common sense and of the land. We know that the quotas are unsustainable as we have seen the populations of species plummet, and we also know that people do not respect the quotas, let alone the law. And yet we joyfully buy their products.

As I've already pointed out, there are a number of alarming trends very likely to upset a precarious balance that nature has evolved for itself. So far I've been vague in how this interdependence affects us, but let me give you the first direct example. In Japan, a country which has traditionally been one of the biggest consumers of seafood in the world, the fishing industry is in the midst of a slow collapse. This collapse is partially down to the simple arithmetic of overfishing. If you remove all the fish, there can be no industry. But this is not the whole story. Off the coast of Japan there is a particular species of jellyfish; 'Nomura's jellyfish', that has gone completely out of control. The reason for this is that in their smallest polyp stage of development, these jellyfish are consumed by the trillions by fish, and in later stages by turtles. The eradication of fish stocks, as well as the disgraceful bycatch eradication of turtles, has meant that there is nothing left to balance out the jellyfish blooms that are exploding off the coasts of Japan.

These Jellyfish are so out of control that they are actually killing each other in their rush for global domination with the scarcity of resources where they are. There has been a dramatic uptick in jellyfish numbers and a dramatic spike in algae growth. When there is a bloom of these creatures, all others suffer. The seabirds that make a huge contribution to the fertilisation of our land are left without food sources, reducing the amount of nitrogen washing up on shore. This lack of nitrogen is starting to become a major problem already, and the soil is degrading in most places faster than we can safely replenish chemically, more on this later. We can do nothing about these jellyfish, and eventually they will be the only lifeform left in the ocean, and then even they will starve. Our ability to fight against them is reduced by our continuing destruction of our only ally in the fight; sea life.

Quite aside from the destruction of fish populations, the saddest part of the death of the oceans for me is the loss of the bigger species, in observed numbers, not industry ones. Now this is a tangent, but it hurts me too much not to mention. Each year more than 300,000 small whales, dolphins and porpoises are killed, by accident. Whales are the most beautiful species that grace this planet, with brains we do not comprehend, with languages and cultures and social patterns that indicate intelligence, and we kill them BY ACCIDENT!? We've banned whaling throughout most of the world and that's great, but it doesn't protect whales from the fishing of other species. On top of this heart-wrenching tragedy, each year 100 million sharks are killed by accident and more than 250,000 turtles are accidentally killed by fishing practices. And literally billions of fish that aren't being hunted are thrown overboard, dead, as they've been accidentally killed, and aren't commercially useful.

This is the most disgraceful and wasteful aspect of human consumption that can be seen on earth, and I'm from a country where we burn the earth itself for our electricity! It is impossible to comprehend how much has been killed and how quickly. We are in the midst of the worst ocean extinction ever seen. The biggest extinctions in our geological history came nowhere near the level of destruction we have wrought on the seas and oceans. I can tolerate ANY level of violence and barbarity in pursuit of the cessation of this onslaught. It doesn't matter how many will starve. It cannot go on. Many more will starve if we don't curb our dependence immediately.

There are so many more individual species' stories to tell. We could talk about the Hawksbill Turtle, the Kiribati, the Labrador Duck, the Great Aulk, the Grayling fish, or the Ealgrass limpet, may they rest in peace. We could mention the polar bears, though they're quickly becoming land animals, and we'll talk about the land in the next chapter. I would love to go into all there is to know about whales. They are spectacular and magical creatures. The largest creature to ever live is a whale swimming in the ocean right now. But we can't possibly talk about all the extinctions and near-extinctions because there are just so damn many. The UN's best estimate is that 1 million separate species face almost immediate extinction in our oceans. About 72 are due to go any moment, or we have already seen the last of. The appearance of a great many species is now only rarely noted.

It is very hard for an individual to square the apparent ultra-diversity we have with the mass extinction we have. I had an excellent opportunity a number of years ago to have this illustrated for me with clarity. I lived in China for a year, and while travelling for the New Year festival I went to Hainan, that massive island off the south coast, for a beach holiday. While there I had the marvelous opportunity, in the land that health-and-safety forgot, to go scuba-diving on a coral reef completely unsupervised. It was amazing. As you have undoubtedly heard before, nothing can prepare you for the miraculous diversity and stupendous beauty of a healthy coral reef. There are more colours than you'll ever see on land and the sheer number of species you observe is incomprehensible. I wandered around underwater for the full extent of the time my tanks allowed, just taking it all in, but unfortunately it wasn't all beauty and wonder.

The section where we were dropped was obviously a healthy and untouched reef and made me want to cry for joy, but swim a hundred metres either way along the beach and what you find is acres and acres of dead reef. After the beauty of seeing what it should have been, seeing the endless bleached-white desert of dead reefs is shocking. I nearly drowned in my immediate reaction to seeing the death of this biome unfolding before me, and partially my incompetence and a dangerous riptide. It is obvious the moment you see it that this is a man-made catastrophe. You can see how the dead reef sections are spread out in a fan from the river that flows through town. Without the colours of a healthy reef, all the rubbish and plastic and oil in the water stand out a mile; the only colour you see is of pollution. At the age of 18 I realised I was looking at the end of the world. I'd love to know if there's any healthy coral left in Hainan. I doubt it.

The destruction of habitats and populations and the brazen disregard for the oceans will cause the world we know to end. Life may go on for a while without the oceans having the wealth of life they've always enjoyed, but will our lives continue in a way that is recognisable to ourselves? For many cultures the consumption of seafood is part of their identity, so in that sense the loss of fish means the end of their cultures. If we allow the delicate balance of predator and prey to be utterly destroyed because of our callousness, then we will live to see the collapse of all sea biomes. When we have algae and jellyfish out of control, we will slowly lose our planets' ability to oxygenate, which may be a slow burner, but we will also lose the world's ability to self-regulate climate changes.

When the oceans lose a large part of their absorptive qualities through the destruction of plant and plankton life, the on-land ecosystem will be dramatically and adversely affected. We are heading full-sail towards this outcome, and I gravely doubt our ability to reverse it, let alone even mitigate the worst effects of it. In the sense of damage limitation, the best outcomes we could hope for is the potential for creating artificial biomes for the preservation of cornerstone species, not a recovery of fish-stocks. Recovery of fish stocks would be meaningless if the biome those fish depend on is destroyed irreparably. And worst of all, I'm not even finished yet; there is another very very scary issue affecting our oceans that I truly see no solution for.

Nuclear waste. You will have noticed if you looked at my depressing table of contents that there are a number of ways in which nuclear waste is going to end our way of life. I will later go on to talk about how background radiation levels have nearly tripled in the space of one human lifetime, and how the effect of our dalliance with radioactive material is absolutely destined for a tragic end, but for right now, let me talk about how nuclear waste affects the oceans. Since the very beginning of human experimentation with nuclear fission, we have treated the ocean as some kind of infinitely renewable and indestructible sphere. From 1946 until now, tens of thousands of barrels of nuclear waste have been dumped into the oceans.

We should know about the famous dumping in 1946 of hundreds and hundreds of barrels of waste produced by reactors and enrichment facilities from the USA, and how when some of the barrels didn't sink, they strafed them with machine gun bullets until they sank. You should know about how 80% of the water used to contain the disaster in Fukushima a few years ago washed away into the sea and spread in a horrible radioactive wave across the entire pacific and beyond. But I wonder did you know that nearly all nuclear-powered countries dumped waste into the oceans, from 1946 until 1993, when it was internationally banned? And that even then it continued off the coasts of countries unable to control their waters, such as Somalia? I'll bet you didn't. I didn't. And I like reading this stuff.

The measure of all the nuclear and radioactive waste dumped into the oceans isn't a quantitative measure of litres or kilograms, but in their radioactive signature as recognised in the moment of dumping. Since 1946, the quantity of dumping of nuclear waste, as measured at the time is 85000 TBq. The Bq stands for becquerels, which are the number of decaying particles of radioactivity per second that are being shot out of the decaying material. The T is for tera as in terabyte. So, the sum of all the nuclear waste dumped into the sea, THAT WE KNOW ABOUT, is releasing 85 million radionuclides per second. This is incomprehensible to you and me, but let me spell it out for you.

The nuclear powers of this world have dumped thousands and thousands of barrels of spent nuclear fuel and radioactive waste into the oceans. These barrels are subject to the same forces of rust as the aforementioned sunken ships. These barrels are due to begin spewing their ridiculous evil into the oceans any moment now (at least those that weren't riddled with bullets on day one) and nuclear waste is oh so very bad for life. One of the most alarming aspects of this whole revelation is that the most radioactive seafloor on earth isn't off the coast of Japan as you might assume, but was in the Irish sea, until we were just pipped by Somalia. The Brits spent a good few years just pouring their poison onto Dublin. It makes me feel somewhat patriotic.

I often ask students of history; "How many nuclear weapons have been detonated in the world?". The morons will quickly think "two!". The more intelligent will think about famous tests and cases and think; "maybe a few hundred". Of the recorded tests, which does not include those done in subterfuge, there have been more than 1,981 nuclear bombs exploded on earth, of which 1,978 were bigger than the two dropped on Japan (all but the first test). These figures do not include all the nations who have illicitly tested their mass-destruction machines and escaped attention, like Israel, South

Africa or North Korea, or any device smaller than the bombs dropped in WW2, of which there is growing evidence of a much larger scale than expected. More are still happening, as I write, even today.

The majority of these tests were conducted on, or in, or very near the ocean. The bikini island atoll near Hawaii has been so irradiated that no human can hope to visit there again for the next thousand years without suffering a seriously inconvenient dose of Leukaemia. Some of the tests, especially by the Americans, were actually conducted in the water. IN THE WATER! The French were terrible for their destruction of coral reefs in their testing, and who knows what effects the Russians had on the arctic circle. There's a lot of nuclear waste in the oceans. The radioactive material that has been released into our oceans in the last 80 years would be enough to destroy the whole land-based world several times over. And still we eat food from the sea.

As if this weren't enough, we still haven't REALLY talked about Fukushima. The reactions in both Fukushima and Chernobyl are still underway. It really takes a very long time for these fission reactions to stop cascading. Luckily for this chapter, Chernobyl is quite far inland, but Fukushima couldn't be closer to the sea without being in it. In the first days and weeks of the Fukushima disaster, there simply wasn't enough water or water storage to keep a constant flow of cooling water running over the remaining reactors at the plant and to control the reaction in the reactor that melted down. So the water was taken from the sea and then pumped back into it. In the following days and weeks, gigantic water tanks were constructed to contain the mammoth volumes of water needed to just about keep on top of the reaction. These water tanks leaked.

Anyone can look at the radioactivity data collected as it spread from the coast of Japan and see just how widespread the irradiated water travelled. Within days, molecules of radioactive material had travelled all around the world. Just google 'fukushima radiation heatmap'. The data for how much health damage it has done has been savagely suppressed by the Japanese government. We simply cannot undo this disaster. It is an obvious fact that the oceans have been even more irradiated than the land and air. We see a doubling of our background radiation walking around on continents thousands of miles from the nearest nuclear explosion, so what must it be like for that one dilute biome called 'the ocean'?

My favourite quote from all the many articles and things I've read of a quasi-scientific nature about nuclear radiation in the oceans is this one:

Super-sensitive instruments detected the cesium, but the fish weren't unsafe to eat. "Just because you can detect it," Fisher said, "doesn't mean it's dangerous."

Yes, it does! Jesus-yes-it-does; you cannot clean or cook off radioactive particles. For some obscene reason governments around the world, or at least sizable chunks of them, are involved in an open propaganda war of disinformation about the contamination and potential containment of nuclear radioactivity into the future. It is not the future of electricity; it's just that a lot of people are so heavily invested they feel there's no turning back and will pay any price, which in the big scheme of things is absurd.

I'll tell you what; radiation is like… really bad man! Radiation is not something we should have toyed with. There are simply no good outcomes long term from having split the atom. There are people, even today, who advocate nuclear power as a potential alternative to burning fossil fuels. This is the most lunatic fallacy of our species; I'd rather have no electricity than continue this fiasco, let me explain why. We have limited supplies of the materials needed to practice nuclear fission, so it is definitively unsustainable. We have absolutely no way of disposing of our nuclear waste and spent fuel rods, and around the world since 1993, nuclear reactors have been simply stockpiling all their waste on top of their reactors (unless they've been illegally dumping off the coast of Somalia of course, which some have).

This means that if there is any further disaster in any of these plants the problem will be dramatically multiplied by all the fissionable material coincidentally sitting nearby, and many are jam-packed. Some may even have to close simply because they're full. Uranium mines that have closed down will continue to leak contaminated material into the water table for millennia to come (the same as with a wide range of horrific minerals by the way). When mines of these radioactive materials are shut down, the companies responsible for them are supposed to put in place and maintain plans for their containment for thousands of years. Of course, once the mines run out of profit and the companies shut down, they simply pour concrete into the hole and walk away. There are simply no good outcomes to be had from our very misguided adventure in fission.

The real problem with this is how it affects life. The oceans will be the first place where we see the inevitable outcome that faces all life on earth because of our crazy fantasy of 'free power'. Let's look at how radiation actually affects life. Radionuclides are particles of various materials that emit high levels of radioactive energy in the form of alpha, beta, gamma and X rays. These particles have such high energy that they can obliterate or severely damage the atoms that make up our bodies and subsequently the DNA that make up our cells. Our bodies have evolved with a certain level of background and cosmic radiation so are in fact very efficient at repairing this damage, but a high dose is a grisly immediate death and a little dose will allow the occasional development of more cancers and other mutations. So, over time, increased levels of radiation directly correlate to increased rates of cancer. Do you want to eat the tumour of a tuna? Even then, the real danger of radioactive material is not to fully formed adults, but to infants and foetuses.

As I'm sure you know, most animal life spawns at a much higher rate and frequency than human reproduction, so the chances for defects and cancers to be present within animal populations is also highly increased. This effect is felt by all living things, not just animals. You might look at places like the exclusion zone around Chernobyl and admire how animal life doesn't care about such danger and will continue to prosper even in disgusting conditions, but don't compare the land with the sea; it is so very much worse in the sea. However flimsy and weak our outer shells are, we land-creatures have a huge advantage over our sea-dwelling cousins; we do not have to ingest the contaminating material in every breath we take, ever mouthful we swallow. We can find fresh growth, untouched by fallout, we can breathe air that has blown in from somewhere clean. The creatures of the ocean have no such option. Every intake of their gills and every swallow they take, contains the diluted remnants of the horrible things that have been done to the ocean.

As I've said, the effect on our oceans of our ridiculous position on nuclear fission will be much more dramatic than it is for us on land for the time being. Within our lifetime, more radiation will spill from those rusting barrels than any human or land-creature has ever been exposed to, as a natural background, and within a matter of days effectively every single ounce of seawater will be as badly affected as every other part of the ocean. For us to continue to eat seafood is absolutely flabbergasting, but I still occasionally won't say no myself! Salmon and prawn are irresistible, even though I know how stupid it is to eat them. I stop today.

It is simply disgusting what seafood has to swim through on a daily basis, and it isn't just our shit and our piss. I genuinely believe that in about 100 years, unless something sci-fi/magical is done, our treatment of the world's oceans will spell the end for all life on earth. I also believe there are less than ten years left of seafood. Not only do we need to stop and prevent the traditional and time-honoured attitudes to the oceans that have been foundational in our cultures, we also actually need to actively de-pollute the oceans in some way if there is to be any hope for anything other than a sterile soup of human hubris instead of an ocean. This is the end of the world, and I beg you to prove me wrong. It only gets worse, young hominid.

2: Collapse of the natural environment

It should be a warning to you, in and of itself, that this section is the second most important section in my book about how the world is about to end. But the oceans are fundamental and deeply connected to everything else; everything depends on a healthy ocean. Anyway, let's move on to talk about all the ways that the biodiversity our society depends on and lives in is about to collapse on land as well as in the sea much sooner than you think. In this section I will talk about some of the really hot-button popular environmental issues of the day, but once again I don't want to talk to you about things you should already know, but point out the effects and inevitabilities you may not have realised yet. If you are in any way paying attention, you will know beyond any shade of doubt that man-made global warming is underway, and if you cannot accept this I invite you to speak not again until you die, though let me simply prove you wrong first.

Some people still say "the science isn't settled", which shows an absolute ignorance about the nature and function of science, but is even colloquially just wrong. There is absolutely a universal scientific agreement that man-made global warming is under way, and that our burning of carbon fuels is the direct cause. The evidence is there to be seen, and the evidence against scant to the point of non-existence. On top of that, the jungles and rainforests are being swept away, and the last wild lands are being encroached. It is baffling to imagine farmers in Brazil cutting down centuries of growth to get one season of soya beans, but there it is; it's happening before our very eyes. You're eating it right now. In so many horrible ways, we are shooting ourselves, not in the foot, but in the heart. I'm not going to waste my time arguing those things to you. If you have the ability to read, you can find this out for yourself. What I would rather do is look at some of the nuances of the implications of what this means for our continued existence.

How much warming are we going to experience and what will we likely witness as a result, and most importantly, do we know for sure? First, we definitively know how much carbon is in the air today, how much carbon was in the air a hundred years ago, and at all other times for hundreds of thousands of years through the study of ice cores, tree stumps and the oceans themselves. For hundreds of thousands of years, the highest level of carbon dioxide in the air was 300 parts per million, and this was rare compared to a normal level of about 100-200. In the last 200 years we have leapt to 400+ parts per million and are steadily rising year on year. We are fairly certain that all fluctuations of temperature throughout history have correlated precisely with the amount of carbon released; in most cases simply as a correlation, but now, absolutely definitely, as a direct causation, perhaps for the first time ever.

We burn more than 96 million barrels of oil every day, and by the way all possible reserves add up to about 1.3 trillion barrels (less than half a lifetime remains, more on this later). We also burn about 8 million tonnes of coal every year, and 3.8 trillion cubic metres of natural gas each year. If we were to stop burning this poison today, it would take a very long time for the natural cycle to capture this carbon, but in truth it simply wouldn't, because we have already long passed the tipping point where the heating is completely out of control, due to the loss of reflective snow, glacial and ice cover, and other feedback effects. Please go back and read those numbers again. You did not fully appreciate them; pay attention to the units of measurement which caught me out at first. We are burning fuel at a preposterous rate.

Since 1880, the global average temperature has almost risen by 1 degree already. This change means that glaciers are demonstrably receding and permafrost is thawing, and the weather patterns are changing. The thawing of the permafrost that has come about because of our activities will continue for decades **no matter what**, and each year permafrost will off-gas more and more greenhouse gases, compounding the heating dramatically. The slight increase in sea temperature also means that the sea's ability to cope with greenhouse gases is reduced. The other disturbances and contaminations of the ocean further reduce its ability to cycle the carbon, so even a continuation of 'normal' greenhouse gas emissions caused by nature itself will feed back and continue to compound the problem. It is simply too late to argue about preventing a catastrophic rise in temperatures. We must do it. There are enormous reserves of methane trapped in various places we threaten that will break free in a cascade of warming very soon. It's speculated by some studies that when a certain chemical tipping point is reached, potentially temperatures could suddenly sky rocket. It is completely unprecedented however.

In the best case scenario, with a global consensus to fight tooth and nail, and to disregard people's desire to improve their material lives, we could hope to see a 4-degree increase in the next hundred years. A 4-degree rise sounds small, but the implications are apocalyptic. And I am extremely sceptical that we will sacrifice people's well-being and happiness for the environment. You'd be mad to suggest it. What we are most likely to see is an uncontrolled death-spiral. Once we break 4 degrees, the next ten comes exceptionally quickly; perhaps as soon as one further lifetime. Your great grandchildren will see summer temperatures reach as high as twelve degrees more than today. I'm talking Celsius, my dear American friends. What I'm saying is; we will not survive unless we act extremely dramatically very quickly.

So far, this 1-degree increase in temperature has melted enough ice for the seas to rise 20 centimetres already. Again this doesn't seem like much, but for Venetians and the people of the Maldives, and some pacific islands, it's already enough to be getting along with. The best conservative/optimistic estimate is that we will see almost one metre of sea rise in the next 80 years. I would like to live through most of those 80 years, so I will see over half the world's population move in my lifetime as a result of sea rise if this highly optimistic prediction is true. I am not optimistic and more realistic studies suggest we will see 2 metres of rise in the next hundred years. It is very difficult to predict how much land will be swallowed by the sea, but we're talking about hundreds of thousands of hectares, maybe millions.

There are more than 50 cities that will be completely under water in a hundred years. On the conservative side of the estimates, 300 million people's households will be submerged, but with a pessimistic eye; up to 75% of the entire human population will be displaced. Every place that builds levies and seawalls will aggravate the problem for everyone else. The richest countries will be able to protect their most vulnerable areas, but at the cost of pushing that land-loss on to somewhere else. There will be an arms race of levy-building. Sewerage systems around the world will be made obsolete. The vast majority of our infrastructure in the entire world is centred around our coastal cities. Needless to say, the increases in flooding we will inevitably see will carry off a ridiculous amount of our worst pollutants. For example, the tsunami in the pacific washed millions of tons of artificial materials out to sea, not to mention all the horrible stuff it washed back onto the land. We must start winning this fight. We cannot contemplate losing.

Although this is terrible, and a tragedy we

cannot hope to avoid, causing a societal meltdown and a refugee crisis on a scale never seen before, this is not in and of itself apocalyptic for all life. We may well come up with solutions to these problems. We may well build huge dikes or reclaim land by dredging the seabed (not great because of all the mercury etc.), and one way or another life will have to go on, but there are other problems with sea-rise that have a cascading effect, to create a perfect cascade that will overwhelm us.

There are very delicate ecosystems that have developed in shallow seas and will be forced to move further up the shore. Corals cannot do this. Even if the reefs can survive the bleaching and destruction from fishing, they cannot survive being buried under an extra 2 metres of water, especially when the 2 metre rise will result in huge amounts of earth and rubbish and sewage being washed onto it. Losing the diversity of our reefs will have a chain-reaction effect on all food-chains on earth. It's truly amazing how many species need the protection of coral reefs in order to develop into reproducing adults.

Further to this, the lands we don't defend behind huge levies will be saturated with salt. Some of the best agricultural land on earth will become unusable, but worse, quite a lot of the most fertile natural land on earth will be inundated. Mangroves around the world cannot bear too extreme a change in too short a time. The areas of land lost to sea rise will have a ridiculous knock on effect on every species on earth. Huge numbers of migratory animals depend on there being particular resources in particular places and have evolved over hundreds of thousands of years to live in symbiosis with those plants. That will be so quickly changed that those species will simply die out. The number of migratory birds that will be affected number in the billions. It's a hard thing to measure, but I would bet that billions of birds being lost, producing the best natural fertiliser known to man, would have an extremely detrimental effect on the fertility of all soils everywhere.

Sea bird nesting sites will also be forced to move, and for some of those species, moving is not an option. Many birds nest in types of sites that have existed at the shores for millions of years, and will not be able to adapt in one hundred. Amphibians and crustaceans who lay their eggs on shore will also move, and again, some of those laying sites have remained in place for thousands of thousands of years, and the ability of the lay-ers to lay is dependent in some cases on the type of surface they are laying onto. If you have lain eggs into sand for millions of years, will your species be able to adapt to having to be buried in soil as coasts are eroded more quickly than nature would expect and new beaches are forged? I hope so. And what of them if we build huge levies and dikes?

The top-soil we have is a precious, and limited resource. Sea-rise will not necessarily directly affect the quantity and quality of all our top-soil reserves, but all parts of the living world are interconnected, and certainly some will be inundated. Top-soil erosion and other effects on the fertility of our land are compounded by sea-level rise and temperature increases due to its finite nature. Further, one of the oft-cited effects of climate change will be an increase in precipitation and the changing of seasonal rainfall patterns. More rain inevitably means more leeching of top-soil. Higher temperatures mean a reduction of the soil's ability to capture and store various nutrients, but also its capacity as a carbon sink.

When soils and dung and decaying matter do not freeze in winter, that's bad and when rainfall is increased at a time when there is no vegetative cover on the land, that's really bad. These two effects dramatically affect soil's ability to absorb and contain the carbon and other nutrients deposited in the Autumn. And these are just the outcomes foreseen by global changes to temperature; that's not to mention the fact that human activity has accelerated top-soil erosion to about 50 times its normal rate on top of all that.

The reasons for this degradation of our most important food resource is to do with intensive farming practices. The more land that is tilled, the more quickly the land degrades. The more land given over to seasonal crops means less vegetative cover in the winter. An uncomfortable truth for environmentalists is that if everyone were to switch to a vegetarian diet, we may actually see an increase in environmental damage in the short term. Fields of grass are better than fields of bare soil in the winter. Although it is true that in this scenario we would need less land dedicated to food production, and tillage would decrease, the fact is that vegetarian farming practices are not necessarily any better for the land itself, and in some ways are worse.

A field with grass cover, used for the rearing of livestock, provides a habitat not just for the livestock, but for a myriad of species, both flora and fauna, that would otherwise be reduced to a mono-culture. It is not desirable or profitable for a farmer growing vegetables to have rodents and other lower-order mammals on their land, or plants whose foliage would compete with the crop. A field of grass, at an absolute minimum, is a habitat for four or more separate species of grass and realistically provides good ground for a certain amount of wildflowers and weeds. This diversity invites a host of insect and animal species to use the habitat. The provision of this habitat for voles and mice gives owls and other predators something to prey on.

A field with only potatoes in it has only got potatoes in it. If there are small creatures living among the potatoes, a sensible farmer will seek to reduce this impact on their crop. Insects and pollinators having only one species to work with lose the variety in their diet that provides them with protections from various illnesses. Ironically, some of the worst and most fragile top-soils are in the seemingly fertile rainforests. People would like to completely blame the deforestation, through slash-and-burn agriculture, on cows, but in fact some of these effects are by farmers growing vegetable crops. In Brazil it is soya and in Indonesia it is palm-oil. When you slash a forest for grazing, you can theoretically, though it doesn't happen in practice, keep a little of the plant life that naturally belongs there, to allow them to recover slowly when the cows move on, but one crop of some vegetables on these poor top-soils is all they can bear before they become dust-bowls. Neither is right, I'm just pointing it out.

I've briefly mentioned the insects, but I cannot adequately explain how quickly and how badly the insect populations all over the world are collapsing. As you might well know, famously in China there are so few surviving pollinators in their agricultural heartlands that there is large-scale hand pollination. This means there are armies of people walking through orchards and fields manually swabbing flowers as there simply aren't the pollinators there should be! But this is not a Chinese problem; this is a global problem. That's a Chinese solution though and will work almost nowhere else.

The worldwide insect population is falling by 2.5% per year and therefore will be in all practical sense completely eradicated in 50 years. The reasons for the collapsing insect population are manifold, and in some cases mysterious, although the obvious common denominator is human activity and pollution. In some of the most polluted and unregulated agricultural societies, the levels of insect collapse are terrifying. Puerto Rico has seen a 98% reduction in their pollinator population and promises to become a barren wasteland in very short order. Where the use of pesticides is ungoverned, we can see a very direct correlation with the infamous bee-death calamity. Where the most humans are, the fewest pollinators can be found.

Another devastating effect on insect population

is in our universal uptake of fast-moving vehicles. Billions upon billions of insects are killed by hitting fast moving vehicles every hour of every day, to such an extent that the biggest 'predators' of insect species collectively around the world are now buses and trucks, and to a lesser extent trains and planes and all things fast. The cost of our industrialised world is not just measured in the carbon output of our exhaust fumes, but in our physical stamp on the world around us. Having watched the time-lapses of satellite imagery of this world over the last decades, any hominid-level intelligence would be chilled by the sweeping dominance of our artifice upon the land. So much of the land has been paved over for our use, and worse, divided into every shrinking islands of nature, in so short a time.

Even a vast reserve of land is impacted by as impenetrable a barrier as a motorway. The cost to all sorts of eco-diversity is radical and genetically alarming. To think that ne'er again will a hedgehog's genetic footprint be found in the generations living two sides of a giant motorway is tragic but not quite as devastating as an insect biome fragmentation. Their genetic diversity is as important to their species as it is to any other. Where it lacks diversity, it suffers from heavy viral death-tolls and lowered resilience. And they live fast, intense little lives.

The combination of pollution, pesticides, mono-culture agriculture, habitat loss and human activity are obviously leading us to insect extinction in general, but specifically in pollinators' extinction. This compounds a problem for all other plant and animal life, as insects are both the bottom of so many food chains, and the pollinators of almost every plant. We do not live in horrible totalitarian states like China where tens of thousands of people can be 'employed' to address this problem, so we will simply approach, and then suffer, a spreading global famine. You will read that and think I am over-dramatizing the situation, but I invite you to do even a modicum of research and reading of people and organisations who are measuring this, and see if you can sleep at night. It's devastating. The bees grab the headlines, but they're just one of a number of keystone micro-fauna whose lives we have endangered with our very recent modern lives. I'll reserve the absolutely tiniest of life forms for discussions of our future health provisions. The problem is so vast here that we must consider further the plight of the medium-to-small sized life.

Everything from the fungi to the earthworms depend upon their shared gene-pool developed over the kilo-millennia. The myriad multiple countless little creatures and insects who live in all the niches of all the flowers and plants and weeds and bushes, which themselves have evolved freely across the land, are being pushed into ever shrinking corners wherever there is the will of free people to develop the wellbeing of their society. Populations of small to medium sized plants and animals simply cannot overcome the barriers we have started erecting in the last century. The agricultural cultivation of the land combined with our engineered infrastructure, in places big and small, have widespread effects on the world around us… eventually. Eventually, the pressure on genetic bio-diversity will result in pocket-sized extinctions with no natural way for the species to re-occupy the niches.

We are too short-sighted. We drain and pollute our groundwater and aquifers, and think it will somehow get better at some point in the future, and that we'll recoup the damage we've dealt to waters whose cycles may be longer than we appreciate (more on this later). Wells dig deeper and deeper around the world into groundwater reserves, and soils are leeching under biomes that are meant to contain different 'god'-given flora and fauna. The plants and animals we share this world with are disappearing. We are deep inside this Armageddon extinction event. The bit of this that's bullshit is Armageddon, not the extinction event. We are the extinction event, not god. The final battle is with ourselves.

We are also too in-awe of how vast and steadfast this world seems, when in relative terms, it is not. Consider the human population (at this point in my writing, the population is 7755331550) and our part to play in it, relatively speaking. You will get to know a thousand people in your life, and many more I hope, but of the thousand people that each of those people will get to know, how many connections do you need to make to account for all of us? A thousand, thousand, thousand, thousand humans are all of us that will ever or have ever lived, so obviously there's some overlap in our network, but this simply means that when you do something good or bad… it matters. When you signal that something is positive or negative or right or wrong, it matters. An accumulation of small effects could have devastatingly wide consequences. The profit and loss account of our collective impact is deeply in the red, and our collective behaviours, of which we individually have an important part to play, are disgraceful.

Much like the sea, almost all life on land is under increasing threat from humanity's sprawl. There are so many different stories of extinctions past and present that it is impossible to comprehend fully. We could spend time talking about the eradication from this Earth of more than 500 species JUST in the last lifetime. The Western Black Rhinoceros, the Caribbean Monk Seal, the Pyrenean Ibex, the Caspian Tiger, the Tasmanian Tiger, the Pinta Island Tortoise, the Barbary Lion, the Schomburgk's deer are but a few of the mega-fauna where the last specimen died in captivity in the last hundred years or so, as we watched. The numbers of species under threat are beyond count. Exactly like with the oceans, even though the number of creatures who have fallen off the brink already isn't a majority number yet, the overwhelming majority are on their way to the brink. The rate of extinction is rapidly accelerating as you read this. We're going to lose between 200 and 2000 species a year this decade, where previously a whole decade might account for just a little more than that. We're going from a 0.01% rate to a 0.1, rising to 0.2 at least the following decade. This is beyond grim for the interconnectivity of all life everywhere.

I reckon you and I might live to see the worst famine in human history, and if it isn't caused by a number of factors I might talk about elsewhere, it will definitely come about sooner or later as a result of our loss of insects and other little creatures that we depend on to pollinate and fertilise our crops, and provide nature with its REQUIRED bio-diversity. I mean the creatures who eat the creatures that secrete the glue that kills the eggs of the creatures who poop the shit that feeds the plant that feeds the grass that feeds the cows that feed you, hominid-type person. And there's really nothing we can do about this. We might have sci-fi solutions for a bunch of the problems in this book that I think are highly optimistic, but technically possible, but for this problem I haven't seen a hint of possible solution. We do not have a good solution; we may have only a…. final solution. Terrible evil irresponsible words to utter if you know your history; I simply and grimly mean we need to limit our population.

In the long-term we will absolutely obliterate ourselves ecologically as a matter of pure mathematical certainty, but we can quibble about the longevity of our survival and thus the excessiveness of how ambitiously you dream of us addressing this problem in the short term. We can try to hold on to as much of our lifestyle as we can, while we can. On the other hand, the more pessimistic outlook I fear we must consider are the tipping points of nature. Perhaps if one of many scales are tipped too far, it could be sudden famine, or a slow dripping decline, where no recovery is possible because we don't even know what essential ingredient it is that's missing, or what tipping-point we pushed, until it is too late. So we must act quickly even if we're not convinced the threat is imminent. You cannot predict when the famine will come, only that it is coming.

Nature is resilient and can recover from hard blows, but humanity's growth is relentless and our blows catastrophic. How far can we push our luck tampering with every little tiny detail of the natural world to suit our consumption needs? How long do you think we'll last if this extinction event continues indefinitely? If the answer is less than forever, we must act now to remedy it, no matter the cost. And there aren't infinite species. I'm telling you we can't expect the status quo to continue very long unless we magic up solutions fast. Surely you can all hear the hoof-beats of famine, pestilence, death and war? Our treatment of the environment will bring about an end to our way of life, if not our lives. Already. And here's the second dose of nuclear radiation.

You cannot present a statistically meaningful representation of the growth of radioactive waste contamination, as it has gone from absolutely zero ever, to more than enough, in the blink of an eye. Obviously there have been some very famous localised contaminations, though probably more than you are aware of. The Americans have plenty of egregious sins to make up for, as do a growing host of other nuclear-armed and nuclear-powered nations. As a direct result, the average background radiation on land around the world has doubled and almost tripled, and obviously gone beyond measure in some places.

Certain levels of correlated rises in radiation dosages are pegged as causation in rises in cancer rates, and not all creatures are big hardy ones like we super-fauna. A child should probably be able to explain how devastating increased radiation dosages are on populations these days, even if nature seems keen enough to ignore it. Of course, all living creatures have always lived in a soup of cosmic and solar and raw natural radiation, and of course one day all places where life can be seen will be cleansed by the perpetual onslaught of an entropy-governed universe. However, the current observable rise is not some unfortunate natural cruelty of the devil or a demon of any colour. It is ours alone. We may yet get switched off by some catastrophic cosmic calamity, but that's no reason to be giving ourselves an irreversible problem.

We have seen a great deal of unfortunate mishaps with radioactivity. The horrible pessimism is this; do we think that's it? Have we done all the damage we're likely to do with nuclear meltdowns and warfare? I will speak of war more later, but of nuclear power it's inconceivable on its own. Even if we were to shut down every single reactor on earth tomorrow, there's nowhere for the materials to go for the next few thousand years. We've already filled some reactors to bursting point with waste and we just keep piling it up.

One of the most contaminated rooms on earth is the now closed down reactor at Sellafield, one of the world's first. It ran for only a few decades and we are, in good faith, suggesting that now and for millennia to come its man-made structure will stand guard after all of us are dead. It is a repugnant insult to future earth-dwellers. We continue to seek to build new reactors and think of them as rational expressions of human enterprise, but I cannot sufficiently express how much they are not. What a stupid way to be carrying on! Maybe Fusion will be the answer, but fission is the worst fallacy of our species. We WILL see more leaks, more meltdowns and more nuclear disasters. I bet you a fiver.

With the inevitable inexorable increase in background radiation, and a multiplying number of sites that are highly contaminated, we will see stupendous amounts of cancers and deformities in certain populations of creatures. Who knows what the effects will be and how quickly they'll take effect. It all depends on blind luck, and we're continuing to stack the odds in a global bet. It seems unavoidable that we will continue to need all the reactors we've got running for at least until the apocalypse, and probably all the proposed ones that

people still want to build. So I make the odds as follows;
- live to see another doubling of background radiation   3-1
- tripling, which now would be getting quite bad for one
lifetime   10-1
- last long enough to be around to protect life from our waste
in 2000 years   100-1
- all-out nuclear war   10-1
At the end of all this I'll give my final shortlist for odds I will gladly offer on how the world might end in my lifetime and joyfully take your bets folks.

Second in likelihood to our ocean's life-biome collapsing on a grand scale in a single lifetime, is the collapse of life on land, and if we do continue the way we have for the past 30 years, we will live to see famine in around another 30 unfortunately. I'm hopeful we'll come up with at least a patch-work of solutions to global warming, but not quickly enough. I'm less hopeful of our ability to prevent the mass extinction we are seeing continue. It is already out of control. We are in the Anthropocene extinction, the sixth extinction event of earth, the man-made extinction. It is hard to quantify in general, but every species on earth; both sea and land almost uniquely among extinction events it must be said, has become stressed by our impact on the world. I've pointed out what I think is the most alarming for continued human life, but in all spheres of life, the rate of extinction is up to a thousand percent faster than it has been throughout most of Earth's history.

The biggest natural extinction events of the past killed between 70-90% of large species over tens of thousands of years. We have had a similar effect on the large species over a couple of thousand, but have also managed to wipe out about 10% of all species of any size, AND the acceleration in the past 500 years has been breath-taking. Our impact on mega-fauna has been spectacular throughout our distant past, but in recent years we are extending the danger of our reach to every niche and pocket, and seeing the results quickly unfold before our eyes. More than 80% of large fauna species, on land and sea, have disappeared in a geological blink of an eye. More than half of all plant species are gone, 15% of fish species and 90% of sea life, with almost every species endangered; we are watching this world and this one bastion of life die.

I would rather expel the 10 million humans living closest to the last remnants of gorillas than see them go extinct. I would watch us all starve to stop whaling. I would condone and support ANYTHING that multiplied the territory and numbers of our mega fauna. No amount of human suffering is undeserved in pursuit of the preservation of the life we have been given sacred stewardship over. We must protect nature from ourselves and each other. That will need to be done violently or stupendously quickly. I doubt we will be quick. We've all gone too soft. Humanity is not worth this.

I'm sorry.

But it's not.

I don't know what will become of us if we don't address this. It is terrifying. I waiver each day between anger, despair and hope. Where there is a will there is a way. That is all I can cling to.

3: Resources

This section is going to constitute a whirlwind tour of our resource-crisis, as the problems I foresee with the continuation of our existence as the apex species of this planet in this regard are really obvious and immediate. The development we've come to enjoy over the last few centuries has been rampant and has been largely due to our newly found capability to extract vast quantities of minerals, fuels and ores from the earth and burn and melt them into wonderful and ingenious creations. Because we are such short-lived creatures we feel that the world we have built over the past 4 or five generations has the nobility of permanence, and that we will never relinquish our hard-won gains and advances. Of course a moment's thought reveals how foolish and prideful we are. In the long scale of history, our new found wealth is a blip in time, a mere aberrance, and we will burn out just as quickly as we grew.

I've already predicted the oil will run out before the end of the century, and the childishly obvious concern with this is how all our many vehicles and machines are powered by petrol, diesel or gas. We're currently trying to convince ourselves that if we replace petrol vehicles with electric vehicles we will avoid this problem but that is simply not going to be the case. Undoubtedly we will use up more of our precious resources in pursuit of building these magnificent machines, and fair play, their existence does try to address one of the coming apocalyptic catastrophes waiting to happen if we do not limit our burning of fuels. But that is only one element of how we have grown dependent on fossil fuels; how we need to burn them at horrifying rates right now. You must address electricity before you have electric cars. We don't just burn them though. We also use them for almost everything else too. And unfortunately, we actually need them. We have a surplus population of about five billion due to oil.

The idea that we can replace our cars, trucks and tractors with electric vehicles supposes that we can come up with a whole raft of new materials and processes that are completely independent from the petro-chemical industry. The renewable electricity we need so much of is produced with machines and materials that have themselves been produced as a result of our petro-chemical experimentation for the last century and have a stupendous carbon cost in production and upkeep. We do not seem to recognise that when the oil runs out, we lose so much more than the fuel in the tank; the tank itself is made of plastic, the lubricated parts of the machine are oiled, the tyres are made from synthetic rubber made from oil.

Look around you and think about what single part of your daily modern existence is not built with the benefits of a petro-chemical industry. The synthetic fire-proof carpets and the synthetic clothing materials on your back and on your bed. The treatments of surfaces in terms of preservatives and colours. The containers of almost all the products you have ever owned. It is all from the petro-chemical industry and all of it is finite. All of it is finite in the short-to-medium term! We are crazy to have built such a dependence.

We need to rapidly wean ourselves off the burning of fossil fuels simply in order to preserve those fuels for our future use of plastic and other synthetic materials and processes we have come to take for granted. And doing that would just be another kind of death sentence, as we've already mentioned some of the fallacy of our use of petro-chemicals. It seems most likely we will continue to burn fuels until we have none left and hope that a wild multitude of alternatives will present themselves. We do not yet realistically have any idea what they will be. Yes; we may outrun the fuel problem in some way, and yes there are alternative sources of oil-like products we could grow, destroying more arable land along the way, but nothing can replace the efficiency of what we will lose in but one lifetime.

If you replace plastic with glass and paper, the environmental strain of reaping, rendering and transporting these resources will be unbearable; especially without the magic of fossil fuel. The debt we are incurring for the next generation is vast and unpayable. We need, and seem to expect, a revolution of our production and consumption habits within a space of time that we have never changed within before. In a culmination of thousands of years of societal development, in the last 200 years we have achieved a remarkable change in our understanding and mastery of the world. We expect to overhaul everything again, from how we eat to what we eat with, in less than 50. Almost every single production process known to man will have to stop or change. The task is nearly insurmountable. Our dreams for the future have fast-approaching finite limitations that are only just beginning to become clear.

From wood to oil to gas to coal to peat/turf to uranium, all of our major fuel sources are finite. Energy in the universe is finite, and our ability to capture it is vanishingly finite, so even the renewable energy sources are finite. Not only that, all of our energy sources incur costs. There are only so many rivers you can dam, and great costs for doing so. There are only so many acres you can dedicate to the production and storage and transporting of solar, wind and tidal energies, and at great costs. Geothermal power is interesting, though costly too. And all the nice renewable energy sources suffer from the major flaw of nuclear too; our impermanence.

We cannot safely predict where the coasts and currents and tides and precipitation and winds will be for very long. Even with geology, we are at the mercy of time if we depend at all on tectonic and volcanic stability. Could we maybe drill deep into the crust to dispose of nuclear waste, and tap geothermal? Would it have unforeseen consequences? We simply cannot safely or efficiently make energy yet, in any way that isn't destructive. We do not yet know enough to even do it very well with the cheap and efficient fuel sources like Uranium and Plutonium without great costs. We barely need very much of them to be able to have all the energy we'll need for a dramatically long time if we could use them safely, and we'll have trouble finding even that much without terrific costs, let alone do it safely.

We will have a very big price to pay for having grown our population so quickly if we hope to have a decent amount of energy consumption continue for any length of time at all really. Also, it is only right and proper that people all around the world aspire to have the best quality of life for their children as they possibly can secure, which means doing everything to acquire the material and technological gains of the world in order to enjoy the highest level of comfort and satisfaction. Everyone deserves a crack at a good life.

Our necessity for more fuel and ore and resources is insatiable. Therefore, we cannot reasonably expect any developing nation to halt or hinder their production of resources in any way. Inevitably, all coal that we think may be extracted for the economic benefit of any given country will indeed have to go ahead unless we wish to institutionalise an international inequality of access to opportunity. We need to find a solution that limits our impact and damage to the world while still accelerating and growing our ability to utilise all available resources. This is incompatible. 404. Reset time. We have irrationally conflicting needs in mind for future resources.

All mooted solutions or approaches for saving ourselves from ourselves are deeply dependent on our use of advanced technologies that require rare minerals. Solar panels and modern turbines require very rare minerals, and those minerals and resources are finite. How long can we reliably expect to exploit sources of cobalt and lithium and lead to guarantee sufficient production of batteries? If the answer is less than 'forever', aren't we in a lot of trouble? We continue to build infrastructure and systems that may well be unsustainable, and depend on resources that are vanishingly finite. This is only a shortlist, but for your quick edification, we are foolish to depend too much on: Cobalt, dysprosium, Yttrium, europium, terbium, neodymium, lanthanum, indium, cerium and even arsenic, all of which are critical elements in our modern communication and energy technology, but whose supplies were extremely rare to start out with.

Aside from those 'rare earths', even our supplies of staple mainstay minerals are not infinite, and the time has come for our species to carefully consider what the best uses of those resources might be. Currently we are simply driven by the market forces, which allows the most trivial uses of these minerals take up a disproportionate quantity of our total supply. It is unforgiveable that people replace working phones with new phones every couple of years without a full and total plan for the recovery of the precious materials that constitute these… fashion accessories... these statements of wealth… these trivialities. A technology I will use if it furthers the goal of stopping their use, paradoxically and selfishly.

We have, in a very short period of time, been made aware of the grand scope of our duty of stewardship over this world and although world religions have been espousing our responsibility to nature for millennia, we have only really recently gotten to grips with what that means. We must actually become the shepherds of the earth. That means that all of our actions, and especially our personal consumption, are really our own responsibility and not that of the government, or giant corporations, though it is also our responsibility to limit theirs. This book is about the end of the world, and in this example especially, we are not going to adversely affect the health of the world by running out of the things we need, but we are going to lose our newly found way of life. And there are many reasons we must hold on.

For the kids of today, losing their ability to use phones and communication technology may as well be the end of the world, because they will have to relearn how to live their lives without this technology. We have stupidly made children dependent on things whose obsolescence we measure in months. We may get 5 or six generations of enjoyment out of the motor-car before it becomes obsolete and inaccessible, but we may only have one or two generations who can access the internet before we run out of the ability to maintain this technological infrastructure. The future is very much in the hands of five and six and fifteen year olds. They have the power right now to change the world dramatically and I suspect they will start to flex that collective strength through a combination of social media and anger, which may not be the optimum way to resolve all this. Do we wish our children to have to fight for their survival? Or do we hope somehow that their lives will be even better than our own and we reach for the stars?

I will explore this in detail later on, but when we think of the 'great filters' of the Fermi paradox, one of the obvious candidates is that technology itself is simply unsustainable, or that free-market economies that foster these advancements cannot govern their utilization effectively. We certainly could not imagine a world where every single adult has the latest gadget, without imagining that world to be sterile. But for the time being, briefly, it is a necessary evil we must bring to bear on the problem. We can communicate a thought anywhere instantaneously. 'Tis miraculous.

Nevertheless, the threats to our 'way of life' are widespread, just like the threats to all living things. One way in which our lives could be irreversibly affected is through the huge changes to our diet that have come, and will probably go again, within a short few lifetimes. I've mentioned some of the dangers to topsoil around the world, but haven't mentioned the possibility of us running out of the minerals and chemicals that we are dependent on for our modern use of fertilisers. 90% of our food-production is dependent on fertilisers derived from our exploitation of mineral phosphorus reserves. Our best estimate for how much we have left is 80 years, and some say we have much less. I would like my unborn son to live for 80 years, wouldn't you? In 80 years or less we need to find a replacement for a chemical whose discovery and usage has boosted our agricultural output in the last century by orders of magnitude. This problem is deeply exasperated by our eradication of species who produce phosphorus, and our wasteful use of our mineral stocks. Unless our population falls dramatically, we have one long human lifetime left before an apocalyptic famine. If we make it that far.

Our most optimistic projection for world population growth is that it will level out between 10 and 11 billion. This is based on the assumption that as quality of life and education distribute more evenly around the globe, everyone will follow the same pattern of population decline we see in the rich nations of today, many of which are now offering financial incentives for parents to have more children. Hungary gives 30 thousand euro on the birth of your third child. I gravely doubt we will choose to do the opposite. Where there has ever been potential for the world to support more people, people have raced to fill those spare seats. And even with this conservative estimate of population growth, there is no conceivable way that all of them can be fed in a fair, equitable and sustainable way. We struggle today to feed even half our people in a sustainable way. Food production in the 21st century is incredibly unsustainable.

We eat food that is picked before it is ripened, shipped across the world in unsustainable vehicles, and then chemically ripened using resources we may run out of. We take water that lands on the ground on one side of the world, soaked into fruit, and consumed on the other side of the world. Our world has evolved to have the dung of its growth dropped within a few scant kilometres of where it was eaten, but now we rarely return the dung to the earth at all! Any objective observer would have to conclude that we are a suicidal species.

We are currently losing between 20 to 50 thousand square kilometres of arable land each year, we expect to watch the sea rise between 1 and 2 metres, and our fresh-water supplies are dwindling fast. We simply cannot support the population we already have for more than one lifetime before we see mass starvation, at most another long lifetime. We may not need to worry about our running out of fertiliser because even if we manage to find a magic supply, we're more quickly running out of places to spread it and water to use it with. Our agricultural capacity has peaked and will now fall quickly.

There simply has to be a population control imposed on the human species, and I would rather we decided to do it ourselves than wait for mother nature to determine our maximum for us. To have our populations dwindle due to starvation is a grisly prospect and cannot but lead to horrific suffering and bloodshed. To have anybody dying of hunger in a world where we waste up to 40% of our production is already an intolerable injustice, and only a fool can think it's going to get better, when literally every single contributing factor would suggest the opposite. PLEASE inform me how this is going to get better. I need it for my sanity; this book is killing me. I have looked, and there are only fantasies, rainbows and unicorns. Genetically mutated food sources may be the future, but I think this is a grim future.

In all other chapters I reserved the nuclear problem for last, but in the question of resources it is only one of many, many, minerals we will run out of and lacks the importance of my next focus; water. Although this planet's surface is mostly water, and we've essentially already had a whole chapter about water, it is yet our most valuable and essential physical resource too. And it is a dwindling resource, despite the fact the seas are rising. There are a number of factors to be briefly outlined; our ice reserves are dwindling, our rivers are contaminated, our reservoirs are vulnerable, our infrastructure is unsustainable and our aquifers are almost universally tapped. Oh and seawater is death.

I think I have satisfactorily described or will describe some of these problems, but it is your responsibility to research further and find solutions to these problems, which I pray you do, before it is too late. There is one problem here however that may have escaped your attention; our underground stores of water, where we mostly actually get the water we use. In most countries the water table has been measurably affected. In India, more than half their wells and aquifers are dropping by more than a metre per year. In Australia, one of the largest contiguous aquifers on earth has lost a quarter of its productivity in the last century, and is otherwise wildly vulnerable to contamination risks due to fracking and mines, both current and abandoned. Ground water is under threat almost everywhere. We will not have enough fresh water for our needs within a couple of lifetimes, almost globally.

But please indulge me while I tell you about a problem much closer to home for me, and one which isn't as fastidiously measured and observed. In rural Ireland, we are facing the same ground-water problems that any industrialised country anywhere is experiencing. I grew up on a rural laneway deep in the most fertile and green and beautiful countryside on earth, where there are about a dozen households and two farms. All along this laneway there is a little stream that runs right beside it. This little stream was a glorious asset to a happy childhood.

We built weirs and dams on hot days. There

were frogs and frog-spawn to rivet the inquisitive mind, and minnows to catch and release and a whole biome of life to be appreciated. In my childhood, the stream never ran dry and we could have boat-races with little skiffs made of plastic bottles or bits of branches at any time. When my father and mother built their house on the lane, our oldest neighbour told my father that he had in fact seen the river run dry in a hot summer, and my father, mother, uncles and other neighbours were astounded by the prospect given how waterlogged our country idyll was. Perhaps once a year, the river might become so clogged with leaves and autumn detritus that its course was laboured, but how could a river that had fish in it ever run dry!? How ludicrous.

Then one year, in the height of an extraordinary summer, I was flabbergasted to find that the river had in fact, in some stretches, stopped running. There were still pools and stands of water all along its course, but for the first time in my life the riverbed was completely dry in a couple of places, for a couple of days. I ran to my father to point it out and was forever thereafter supremely alarmed that this was happening, but that older generation shrugged it off at first, remembering what old Tom had told them when they were young. But it got worse.

Now, for much of the year, the river runs completely dry. The extent of the drought means that now there are no pools and eddies that preserve the life of the river, for when the rain returns the stream to its proper working function, there are no minnows, frogspawn or frogs. There are three months or more each year where that stream is nothing but a dead ditch at the side of the road. Now that we are starting to realise that our scant dozen or so houses are having such a dramatic impact on the landscape around us, it is too late to reverse the damage.

Each of us has our own independent well with which to extract water from the underlying water-table. When my father's generation were building their houses, they drilled down 50 to a hundred feet in order to have a constant supply of cold fresh delicious water (and it is the cleanest, most delicious water you can imagine). Now my generation are building houses there and drilling between 250 and 500 feet to ensure we have a good well. And all of this is one of the most rain-soaked countries on earth.

It was unimaginable only a short time ago that Ireland would ever have trouble replenishing its water supplies and reservoirs, and therefore we did not need gigantic water stores to ensure there was a near infinite supply of cool fresh water. Now even in a mediocre summer there are hose-pipe bans for people tapped into the public water supply and each year boil-notices apply to some supplies, here and there. If tiny little rain-soaked Ireland is suffering in this way, what sort of hell-scape must the people of traditionally dry places be facing? The droughts that I have seen in my lifetime around the world have been incomprehensibly devastating.

Australia is burning because of the extensive year-on-year drought that has left its brush like tinder. Sub-Saharan Africa lives from one devastating drought to the next, with plants and animals and people all suffering equally. We are seeing an acceleration of desertification around the world, despite the fact that we are actively resisting this with all our might, and even more alarmingly, despite the fact that world precipitation is actually increasing. I see this as an insoluble conundrum. We will have to build some mind-bogglingly large desalination plants, creating an enormous energy demand, and we have to manage every drop of what we have and it seems we can do neither.

There is still one more resource to talk about though, which is time. Our most precious resource, as living beings who will one day inevitably not be, is time. There is no heaven or hell. We are stuck here in this reality, with only the knowledge we have gleaned through scientific observation and experimentation. Once your life is over, it is over. You have between 0 and 100 years to do, think and feel all the things you will ever do, think or feel. And our time is running out. It is not a revelation of some crazy desert-hermit that has revealed the certainty of apocalypse and not just the name of a great song; it is our rational and scientific achievement as a collective to know the truth of our coming extinction.

We know instinctively that all things must end, and I think almost everyone, except the poor people who still believe in any specific religion, knows that the world always lives on a terrible knife-edge. We are absolutely bound to be wiped off the earth eventually, one way or another. Whether that is by an asteroid or by a super-volcano, by a solar-flare or an unfortunately close supernova, it doesn't matter; extinction is a certainty. What does matter is our supremely unique ability to realise this. In all the observable universe, nothing else seems to be remotely able to off-set the horrific entropy of the hostile cosmos. We have an obvious and almost miraculous ability to foresee and resolve problems that are coming.

Even if you completely reject the morbid thrust of this book and write me off as a mere angst-ridden conspiracy theorist, that still does not excuse us for our inactivity. Even if global warming weren't happening before our very eyes, we would still be better off seeking a way to live without fossil fuels. Even if you thought that some 'god' had provided us with this whole world and universe, you should still surely think it cannot merely be a prison for us to live on until the very end. Even if you reject every single threat I think will quickly destroy us, you should still see that our present way of utilising nature is obnoxious and disgusting. You should still understand unsustainability.

It doesn't matter if you think the oceans have some infinitely magical capacity to bear our continued onslaught, because even if they did; what we have done to them is disgraceful anyway. It doesn't matter if you think our extinction event will turn around, because we should be trying our best to multiply and strengthen the life in our care anyway, even if it were already prosperous. Even if you have some deep optimism and admiration for humanity's capacity to overcome our problems, you must surely be ready to admit that we are currently not. And if not now, when? If not now, when!? I absolutely despise the grating of times' sands; as it glacially erodes away our remaining time on this earth, both individually and collectively, but it is made all the more excruciating by how trivially we regard our time. There is no afterlife! We only have now!! We have a time-limit and I whole-heartedly believe that time-limit is fast approaching.

This is not a test.

I'm not just trying to be offensive. I'm trying to get everyone all together all at once to work towards our survival. It is a mountain I will try to climb and hope others will too. Let's climb this mountain. Only this side of it is ugly. The promised land of prosperity and plentitude seems almost within reach. We are so close and yet so far. We must awaken.

4: Health Hazards

(I wrote this before covid 19, but have left it largely unchanged. This outbreak merely highlights our vulnerability in a global age further. Others will write rampantly about Covid. I'm already tired of it. It's not our first, it's not our last. Read on.)

Since we're talking about all the ways in which human civilisation is facing collapse in a few short lifetimes, it would be remiss of me not to mention all the ways in which our short-lived bubble of medicinal advancement in the last century will soon burst. This is really less how nature will be affected by us, but how we are going to be affected by nature. To be honest, the fact that humans are facing some unfixable medical problems is a blessing for the rest of the living creatures left after us, and so I'm not too worried for ourselves; more for the rest. That being said, we know not what we have wrought on this world with our hygiene and medical advancements in the last century.

We were governed by absolute ignorance in our understanding of biology and health until very recently, and now that we've managed to peel away a few flakes of our ignorance, we think of ourselves as the masters of the microbial, viral and infectious. We are far from it, and even as we rapidly accelerate our understanding and applications of that understanding, nature is against us. We are now almost bringing about more new health hazards than we are solving. We think that because our 'life-expectancy' has gone up that our health and well-being has gone up. It's like we think that no one lived to be 80 before we had modern medicine.

Of course people lived to be just as old long ago as they do now. The only difference is we are now individually much more unlikely to die prematurely. The largest expansion of our life-expectancy has nothing to do with our management of the latter half of our lives at all, but everything to do with how we begin our lives. Until very recently, the numbers of children and mothers who died in childbirth were astronomical. The rate at which young children succumbed to an early death, after birth, was unbelievably excessive too. It is wonderful that we have made child-bearing so much safer, and almost miraculous how we have eradicated a lot of health-hazards common to our children. And these have more than doubled our AVERAGE life-expectancy statistics. That is not an extension of life by any means.

It was recently said by a Nobel laureate that the first person to live to a thousand may have already been born, which is absolute codswallop. There have been countless demonstrable cases of historical figures living long past our current life-expectancy at times when our knowledge and understanding of how biology and health was absolutely zilch, or worse, we actively harmed people the moment they fell ill. Methuselah was probably about eleventy-one years of age like Bilbo. The uncomfortable truth of our health paradigm is that we may in fact be living less well in the second halves of our lives than we did before, even though we have better treatment and understanding than ever before.

It is often said that if we all lived forever, then everyone would get cancer sooner or later. This may well be true, but that is not to say that cancer, and especially causes of cancer, are not increasing. When we removed the death sentences that came with various diseases and infections, it is certainly true that other causes of death like cancer and heart disease rose in their place, as all things must die eventually, and usually something kills us. However, we have definitely increased the possible causes and aggravations of cancer and heart disease dramatically too. Not to mention the stupendous rate we kill ourselves with vehicles.

It may simply be a symptom of our better

diagnostic ability that no one ever seems to die of 'old age' these days, but it seems to me that many people suffer a great deal, for a greater portion of their lives, than before. The way that most of us will die in the rich countries of the world is on a hospital trolley, in tremendous pain or in a dull drug-induced stupor. This may somehow seem better on paper, but in the ugly reality, we all know that end-of-life care is a growing concern worldwide. It is astounding that we mostly still live in societies where euthanasia is illegal when we also live in societies where we know our deaths will be in suffering. We have bought into a fantasy of technological medical utopia, even if it costs us dearly.

But none of this is apocalyptic, merely miserable. The really horrible bit is that we also seem to doing irreversible damage to ourselves and the living biomes around and in us in our pursuit of these miserable drug-flavoured deaths. Until a century ago there were no allergies. Of course people will leap to say it is part of our medical advancement, and that people most likely suffered allergies without any relief since the dawn of time, but I'm afraid this simply isn't true. There is insufficient evidence. If people had suffered the allergies we suffer today, people would have simply died out.

We do not know the cause of the allergy explosion that is ripping through our population, but we can have a few educated guesses based around the activities we have been engaging in since allergies seem to have come about. It certainly cannot be genetic as those genes would not have survived. It certainly cannot be a simply natural result of our global exposure to different food-stuffs, because how did the Europeans survive the Columbian exchange? What we can say with some certainty is that some way in which we have started to treat our environment and foodstuffs and even our bodies in the last century has caused the birth of allergies and the exceptionally fast rate of their propagation.

What could this possibly be? Well there are a

number of ways in which our use of land and contamination of food sources could very easily be to blame. We've already explored how universally we are consuming man-made chemicals and minerals on a daily basis. This alone must surely be having an effect on our long-term biological well-being. In fact, we know it is in certain isolated cases. We are well aware of the widespread contamination of our food, both by incidental pollutants, and by contaminants we wilfully imbue our food with. From fertilisers to pesticides, from chemical treatments, to chemical leaks, to radiation in the ocean, what we allow to happen to our food before it crosses our lips is astounding.

We have become almost completely detached from the endeavour to grow or capture food, which was our over-riding preoccupation for aeons, and we allow foreign actors who are ostensibly our enemies to provide us with the food, seed or fertiliser upon which we depend. For any of our billions of ancestors, the idea that we would accept food blindly, on trust, when we've had no hand in its preparation, is wildly irresponsible. How such a drastic change in how we source our food has come about so quickly smacks of hubris. We think what we've built is so great we can afford to completely abandon our self-reliance. And what's worse, we don't even pay our farmers well for doing it all for us.

We expect our agricultural output to continue in its ultra-heightened productivity forever, and we barely make it profitable enough for farmers to continue, let alone do so in a measured way that puts the true wealth of the land before the economic output. So of course it's no surprise at all that farmers around the world are forced to over-use fertilisers and pesticides, are forced to practice slash-and-burn agriculture, are forced to pump our livestock full of antibiotics and hormones, and are forced to viciously limit bio-diversity in and around their cultivations. We will see a decline in food production within ten years even if we ignore all the other problems. All of this is leading us to a very dark place collectively. The land is being ravaged globally and it is affecting our health already. Something within the field of pesticides, fertilisers, hormones and antibiotics is having a dramatic effect on our health, through their promotion of allergies, cancers and most alarmingly; the destruction of our microbial biomes.

We are dishing out savage damage on our gut-microbes, who basically constitute more of us than we do ourselves. You are mostly a bag of microbes, more than you are a human being, and we have very little understanding of how our micro-biomes both on and in our bodies are vital for our continued health. I have a deep appreciation for how terrific our scientific advances have been recently, and how our understanding of basically all things is rapidly expanding, but we are only very recently considering the welfare of the tiny microbes living on or around us and are just scratching the surface, no pun intended.

We are absolutely inundated in a microbial world. We do not yet have a full conception of how stupendously vast and diverse life is on the tiniest of scales, and not the faintest clue as to why or how. Literally everywhere we look we find new species of microbes and germs and viruses and so on, and we have nowhere near a clear picture, not even a corner piece and a bit of the side, of the microbes we have all got, or the microbes we need, or the microbes we should have and don't. Or won't. Most of what we know about our internal microbial life is what we observe from the faeces of athletes. What we do know is that we've declared war on them in the last century, and they are proving surprisingly robust in their evolutionary adjustment.

Penicillin was a wonder-drug at first, and slaughtered infections, along with the 90 or so subsequent antibiotics that were discovered, but now penicillin is widely ineffective and even widely allergenic. In less than a hundred years. Our newer antibiotics will fare no better in the long-run either though, because it is the rapidity of microbial evolution that is making them obsolete, not their inherent flaws. Drug companies have largely stopped developing new ones too, as the trend is too obviously against their successes in more than the short-term. Get ready to die from splinters once again. That might seem slightly hyperbolic, but a great many people were killed from infections from the most innocuous cuts and pricks only a lifetime ago. The reason the microbes are evolving so quickly in the ways that they are is because of us, plain and simple, and all the many ways we are attacking our microbial world.

We meat-eaters have just about doused our world in antibiotics, and hormones. We have daily slaughtered vast hordes of microbes with our newfound chemicals and medicines and disinfectants, and a newfound appreciation of hygiene. We surround ourselves, and ingest, substances that reap havoc on microbes that could never have reasonably expected to have to cope with a sterilisation of their environment. How fastidiously do you ensure that no soap or detergent or disinfectant enters your gut-biome? And what of the farmers, distributers and processors of your food?

Not only do we clean our kitchen surfaces with our chemicals, but we spray the land and pollute, so there is a massive arms race underway on the microbial level as the survivors propagate, as well as a continuous eradication of microbes that can't deal with us, whether good or bad. Every time you take antibiotics you are killing untold numbers of microbes, but those who survive will be just as determined to kill you eventually anyway, and they may have learned your tricks. Microbial life will always bounce back, because it lives such short, furious lives, and multiply so much. We are actively and increasingly encouraging the microbial life that comes back or survives to develop resistance to whatever we use to kill them, if it can, and we are removing any and all microbes that are protecting us, serving us and maintaining us. Hygiene kills as much as saves, or it will do long term.

And we are under grave threat from the microbial world too. It's not as simple as the headline-grabbing MRSA bug. We are exceedingly unlikely to have seen the last of the great flus or viruses of a more banal variety. (like two months before C-19 broke, I wrote all this) And when we do get one on the scale of the Spanish flu of early last century, it will undoubtedly be exasperated by our lack of microbial resistance and diversity, or by its own developed resistance to our treatments. And it will be hastened by our globalism. The chances of us accidentally eradicating, accidentally creating, or accidentally unleashing a critical microbe or microbes is overwhelmingly high, if we haven't already done it several times over.

That's not even to mention the purposeful and intentional creation of life-ending, genetically engineered plagues and chemical weapons by our friends and allies and foes alike. If I had enough money, I'd probably be trying to cook one up myself! What about a virus to lower the population unilaterally? Wouldn't that be nice!? This is what I imagine someone somewhere is thinking. I'll give you more on this later. I wouldn't be able to do it myself. I care too much about life to think it can survive without us humans forever. We're the species that's evolved enough to ensure life could potentially live forever, even if it's just a box of microbes floating around the universe. We're fighting life at its most fundamental form, when in fact our destiny may be to save them. The microbes may have grown us as conveyors of life to the stars, potentially. We may be the only dot of life in the whole screaming universe, which gives an absolutely obvious prerogative and even responsibility on a spiritual level to populate the heavens. But I'm getting ahead of myself.

In my lifetime, we may or may not see a terrible plague or virus, but we are certainly prepared for it. There have already been a number of pandemic scares. We have a medical capacity unlike any before, and even though it's straining heavily under our aging and growing population, it is becoming very advanced meanwhile. We should be better positioned than ever to face down a devastating illness globally… but one day we will have to. It is sad, but inevitable, and survivable. It is not so certain though, when you take into consideration any combination of aforesaid threats to climate and environmental balances. And these flus will never stop coming back. And even bigger one will come.

Global temperature increase and all that entails does not bode well for our health. The heatwaves and droughts experienced in the last few summers in Europe would have been much more devastating not so long ago. It will continue. And it won't just be heat, it will be extreme weather events happening more frequently due to increased precipitation and disruption of currents and wind patterns we depend on, all with sea rise. We have no idea how far things will really go if we were to even turn off everything tomorrow. It could very well be that we have already tipped it so it will at least reach a five or six degree change before settling back down, and who knows how long that will be; centuries at least. That may be a slow burner, but it will burn quicker and higher the longer we go on as before. That heat will really kill us.

We are already seeing heatwaves kill off tens of thousands of elderly Europeans each summer, in ever-increasing records in the richest countries in the world. Nearer the equator is mostly already a lot of desert, but it's becoming more of it every year. The heat will hurt people closest to the equator most. The ice-caps will melt and the sea will rise, and there will be floods. The flooding and contamination will result in grave illnesses, and the heat will hurt people, directly, I repeat, everywhere. But so might the cold in Europe. We've seen the movie 'the day after tomorrow' and understand that it's a dramatic bullshit thing, but it's a dramatic bullshit thing based on a few scarier non-bullshit things like the gulf stream changing direction ever so slowly or the potential for the arctic cyclone to break loose in the winter, again due to increased precipitation, heat and sea-rise. Brutal winters like Russia or Canada, but baking summers, may go hand in hand. We don't know, but we do know we are heating up the atmosphere faster than it has ever seen before, except perhaps directly after an enormous asteroid.

Won't it be great fun seeing where the dice fall? One sure thing is human capacity to survive 40-50 degree summers, which is this; if you're not rich, you can't. I don't think other mega-fauna fare much better. It will be testing in so many ways that are unimaginable; refugees, famine… and a strain on health capacity. If we allow poverty and inequality to continue to skyrocket, while we continue to live jet-setting lifestyles, squalor coupled with globalism will inevitably cook up a plague or outbreak that will devastate us all. Squalor will be increased with flooding and land contamination, and especially by damage to our water and sewage infrastructure. Sea rise and our mistreatment of fresh water will inevitably exasperate our difficulties in maintaining the health gains we have made in the last century. Then a big virus will come.

Our vast number of contaminants will also strain our future ability to handle health crises. We have exposed ourselves to a wild array of chemicals that have unknowable effects on our health and long-term well-being. We all know how the effects of thalidomide were discovered when thousands of babies were born with deformities, but what if the effect of any single chemical or drug takes longer than one generation to reveal themselves? Most of the chemicals and drugs we take or use today have been invented inside one or two human lifetimes. We simply do not have any clue what the effect will be on our third, fourth and fifth generations of exposure to plastic, chemical cleansers and antibiotics. When testing chemicals and drugs in the most rigorous and responsible ways, we still cannot possibly foresee what the long-term effects may be.

When CFCs were first invented, it was discovered that they didn't have any detectible health effects on people or the environment, which looked great, so we filled the world with machines and products that used them. After a while we figured out they were destroying the ozone layer. We are, quite rightly, proud of our recognition and universal banning of CFCs, but we shouldn't pat ourselves on the backs too soon, because although we have halted the man-made hole in the ozone layer, we have not replaced it or taken steps to restore it. The whole world lives with an increased exposure to UV light mostly as a result of our short-lived love-affair with CFCs, and will continue to do so for the foreseeable future. I'm not saying that everything we've ever invented is evil, but surely some of it is. We can only wait and see.

I wanted to wait for a couple of things to come out that might update us on the hole in the ozone layer, but if anything now, we know less than we did before. It shrinks and grows throughout the year. The only post-corona addition to this chapter is to say that the lockdown seems to have helped the ozone tremendously. Funny that. It's looking like we're finally on top of it, but I suspect only momentarily. I am paying attention closely. We were successful in our collective effort to remove the worst and most egregious attack on its composition, but we haven't removed them all. We can't until we stop producing new chemicals every few minutes, each of which has the potential to break the world in a new and marvelous way. The hole in the ozone layer increases our rates of melanoma in the northern hemisphere. It won't cause the apocalypse if we let it grow again, but it's still there. There is only one way in which to reliably allow it to heal; humans must reduce their industrial and chemical activity instead of growing the economy at all costs. It is so screamingly obvious that our continued way of life will impact our health in the long run in an intolerable way that it is simply unacceptable we permit this to go on.

I once again come back to nuclear waste and

radiation. At this very moment, and every other waking moment of your life from now until you die, you are being penetrated by untold numbers of signals and varieties of radiation. Everything from radio to phone signal to wifi has been created in a very short period of time. We have gone from living for aeons with only the natural radiation of the sun and the cosmos, to bathing permanently in a whole spectrum of energies. Each has been tested for its effects on humans and found to not be harmful, much as the CFCs and thalidomide first presented themselves to be. But has anyone considered where the limits are? It may be fine to live with a permanent signal made by one cell-tower, but we are living in an ever-increasing sea of signals. Just how many wifi signals is your body capable of picking up right now? Look at your phone and notice how many there are.

Everywhere you go in the modern world is awash with radio waves, and although I'm not quite ready to suggest we all wear our tin-foil hats, I will not be convinced that there is absolutely no effect on our DNA, our microbes, or our environment that we have yet to realise. I often wonder about the brand new stupidity of all of us everywhere sleeping within reach of our phones. I hear urban myths about people who sleep with their phones under their pillows finding they have increased cysts and growths, but I've seen nothing seriously proposed yet. I wish I could find something solid on this for this book, though I have read speculation about it. But I'll bet you a fiver: there will be more discoveries of how our modern technology have devastating effects on the world around us. However, we will continue to increase our technological reliance until we are forced not to.

For example, we cannot conceivably NOT build all the nuclear power stations that are proposed to be built, which is an insane position. It looks as if we will need far more of them if we are to reduce our carbon footprint quickly enough. We do not know what will become of all the waste sitting in the current ones, and the closed-down ones, let alone the new ones we will create. We do not know what the long-term effects will be if we merely continue as we are now with a more than doubled level of background radiation. We do not know what will happen to our environment from what we've already let happen, let alone what else will inevitably happen.

It's certain we'll find ourselves rueing the day we split the atom or started burning fossil fuels, but we cannot truly yet say that day has come in health terms. Who knows what the effect on us will be from all the carbon we've released? We have been talking so far about the first apparent effect, which is on global temperatures, but does anyone have a clue what will happen to our long-term health as a result of breathing in much more carbon-dioxide than we have for thousands of years? And carbon dioxide is only one of many toxic gases increasing in our atmosphere each year. Will this have consequences for our health, or the health of the creatures we share the earth with? We don't know yet, but it almost certainly will. The only comparable event would be the end of the carboniferous period where a massive plant life extinction basically created a lot of the carbon fuel we burn today in fairly short order geologically. And when will it be too late? It appears it will be too late at current rates within ten years; that is the global consensus according to best UN data. Hold onto your knickers.

The one thing everything in this chapter has in common is this; we cannot return home again. We cannot go back. We must go forward. The only solution to future health hazards and pandemics lies in our technological mastery of the world. Even if some 'god' returned us to the stone-age, the damage has been done. We have now gotten on the horse and we cannot afford to be bucked off. If we are forced to abandon our technological advancements, we may as well completely give up and succumb to the apocalypse anyway. The only bright future that is, I think you'll agree, palatable, is one in which we figure out all these problems. We cannot allow our health and wellbeing to diminish at a time when we need our strength and resilience most of all.

We must substitute every harmful or polluting activity with another less harmful one. We must seek to counter all the problems we face in such a way that doesn't cause further unnecessary suffering. We must find a way to recycle without asking thousands of our poorest people to expose themselves to disgusting squalor, as I have seen with mine own eyes. We must replace plastic with new products and chemicals, and try to predict the future way in which these substitutes will affect us before they do. We must replace our energy diet with clean and sustainable alternatives while still expanding our energy equity; bringing electricity to the masses. To dream of anything other than an ever-expanding technological future is to imagine a terrible dystopian inhumanity being inflicted on those who can't defend themselves. We will force squalor on billions as hopes for development and advancement are ripped away from developing societies, which will have a heavy health-toll. That may be a choice we have to make in the long run, but it can only be resisted today. A hell where a tiny minority are the only ones able to enjoy healthy lives is not worth the effort and yet it is what is slowly happening in this world already.

What I fear is that we will not outrun whatever health hazard is coming down the line, whether that's a pandemic, or a contamination we recognise too late. We are introducing and necessarily must keep introducing new substances and products whose long-term implications are unknowable until we meet them. I can easily imagine a situation where everyone on earth is forced to consume iodine or something else in order to maintain health levels that can be coped with, by even the richest health-systems on earth. I foresee a situation where a virus or pandemic runs out of control and kills a substantial portion of our population. We are living with an environment increasingly filled with carcinogens and allergens, and I can easily imagine a future where the richest will depend on medical intervention to maintain their lives while the poorest suffer.

I predict a future in which our health outcomes will not get better, but worse. We are already living in a time when more of us will suffer terminal illnesses than ever before, but I cannot imagine a way we will triumph over the natural decay of the flesh. What I can see is a larger and larger proportion of us living in old age and ill-health with a shrinking proportion of young healthy people to bolster our economy. We don't actually need any terrible outbreak or chemical spill to make our health systems redundant; we need only continue to age and proliferate as we are currently. Our great financial systems of social provision were built for a population where only a minority made it to the upper-reaches of life-expectancy, and we are beginning to see a top-heavy health spend that is thoroughly unsustainable unless we imagine, as Japan does, that robots and technology will take care of the problem. They won't. Not soon enough; certainly not soon enough for Japan, who will finally have to open their borders as a result.

It would be remiss of me not to mention the nuclear problem once again, just briefly. In my father's lifetime background radiation on earth has more than doubled as a result of our activities, as I've said, but the most compelling evidence of our own stupidity is the indelible mark man-made radiation has left. The disasters we have witnessed, along with the outrageous testing of bombs in the last century, and the dumping of tons of radioactive waste have created a world that is unrecognisable to science. We are living in the immediate aftermath of an event that will be geologically evident for millennia to come; functionally forever. Since the proliferation of radioactive emissions, we have irredeemably changed and damaged our ability to carbon date. All life on earth has had its signature changed so that future archaeologists will not be able to use the same methods of carbon dating that we do today due to the contamination we've caused.

That we have made a geological impact in one lifetime is absolutely mind-bogglingly remarkable. We will be as detectable to future archaeologists, in these few decades of activity, as the layer of ash that represents the extinction of the dinosaurs. Our impact in one lifetime will forever be the point at which things come before, or after, scientifically and archeologically; 1945 to be precise. And our health will be affected increasingly as time goes on. There is nothing surer than the increase of radiation we will unleash in the future, which will mean more genetic mutations and cancers within all populations of life. We may be able to take iodine for a period to mitigate the effects of future radioactive contaminations, but our slugs and worms and insects cannot. The damage we have already unleashed will take several thousand generations to be fully realised, and we simply do not know how much we can bear in the long run. There are too many health threats approaching all at once.

It seems the universe is empty of life, against all probability. Either we soon discover microbial life living in every nook and cranny of our solar system and conclude the issue with life is getting up into complex forms, OR we discover that everywhere is absolutely sterile, as it currently looks, and that therefore the universe itself is not conducive to life at all, never mind this glorious complexity. Either way, the odds of our maintaining healthy biodiversity and complex life are stacked heavily against us. So instead of inflicting further danger on the life we have around us, it is our sacred duty to preserve and propagate it at every opportunity. Until the moment when our contribution to the environment is a net positive, then I am utterly convinced we are on the path to biological extinction, which seems to be the universal norm. It will take an exceptional leap of our collective technological and ideological capabilities to just avoid our self-destruction, and the time for change is past immediate. We must couple our technological gains with an ethical ideology of growth (shrinkage rather than growth). We won't quickly enough or universally enough of course, so it is to arms, I fear.

Even though we need them, we cannot simply continue to introduce more and more advancements without any clear idea of where we are going, or hoping to go. What's the point of working towards protecting us from a pandemic when perhaps that pandemic is the only thing that's going to save us? We cannot infinitely continue to introduce more and more energy sources into our environment without expecting at some point to have an effect on that environment. We must limit our growth until we have a plan for how to sustain it. We must not invent new communications technologies when all we do with them is trivial, and their effects on us are unknown. Do not be fooled into thinking we have a clue what Pandora has in store for us.

We have recently begun to scratch the surface of real understanding of the world, and our glasses are rose-tinted by statistical increases in our well-being, but we don't really have a clue beyond an ability to say that this generation has wealth and capability beyond the wildest dreams of any previous generations. We are not necessarily any healthier or happier, and even if we are, no one knows if it will be short-lived or permanent. It seems unlikely to be permanent. It seems likely to be very short-lived. Unlike us. We will live for decades past the point where we live in health and happiness. I don't want to spend most of my life being old, and this is what we wish upon our young folk when we consider their life expectancy; you will be old and sick longer than you will be young and fit. We must always make the best of now.

We must stop humanity, and yet preserve our humanity. We must make foes of ourselves and yet do everything to preserve what's best of ourselves. More on this at the end. You will not like my revolutionary solutions in all probability, but I assure you there is no other way to prevent the apocalypse than limiting our population. We must act very soon, or we will be forced to act very harshly. We must stop our growth. And I do not want to sacrifice my wellbeing to do so. Therefore, it seems likely we will have to fight, whether we instigate it or not. We have not yet seen the end of war.

5: I just don't trust us

A lot of what I've spoken about here will be easily countered by people pointing out all the wonderful and inspiring ways in which humans are rising to the challenges being presented to us. There are fantastic geniuses out there working on systems and technology that would blow your mind. There are people who are making hydro-carbon fuel by sucking the carbon out of the air and converting it into renewable and non-polluting fuels. There are people making new plastics and alternatives to petro-chemicals from plants we never thought to cultivate before, and there are so many new ways of making electricity being developed that you cannot help but be a little optimistic.

We are making sweeping changes to our diets and consumption habits and are even inventing ways to clear up the mistakes we've previously made. We might take more pollution out of the ocean than we put in one day in the far future! Very soon the first fusion power will come online with its super-clean, near-infinite energy!! We are geo-engineering the environment; creating clouds and particulates to reflect away sunshine and to control the weather, and we are doing this successfully! We will make things that are astoundingly futuristic and whose creation could not have been imagined by the most brilliant sci-fi writers of only a generation ago. These things are reasons for hope.

But equally, these advancements are cause for despair because we not only desire these super-futuristic inventions, we NEED them. We have put ourselves in a position where we are dependent on the benign actions of all our most technologically and financially advanced people to save the environment. But many of the most advanced people are not benign. In fact, in the last century, quite a lot of our scientific advancement has been achieved by our malignant nature. We didn't split the atom to make electricity. We didn't lace our cows with antibiotics to ease their suffering.

There are large numbers of people whose intentions are anything but benign towards the way of life I enjoy; whole cultures and nations are indoctrinated in hatred. As I've previously mentioned, China might be the best positioned super-power of any to achieve the necessary change to their environment and resource-usage that we hope for, but if China is going to take the lead then I'd nearly rather we failed. We may hope to engineer the weather itself in order to help us save the climate we depend on, but you can be absolutely sure that if a nation like China, or Iran, or even the USA or Russia, were in charge of such an endeavour, they would use it to damage their rivals and competitors. They would, and do, use their power to further their own perverse ideologies. Very few countries on earth have widely held ideological or spiritual attitudes that are compatible with the future we must seek to bring into being, if election results or lack thereof are anything to go by.

If there is a way to increase or decrease precipitation, reflect away sunlight in order to affect global temperatures, or to suck the carbon out of the air and store it somehow, it is certain that this will be done by one group in order to gain an advantage over another, if not simply for money. If India could prevent rain from falling on Pakistan and Bangladesh, they would happily watch them starve. If China were to become carbon-neutral, you can be sure they would use it as a grounds to attack and destroy the economies of the other super-powers, or to undermine their moral high-ground as democracies or defenders of liberty. It won't be long before they have the moral high ground after their years of one-child sacrifice and an objective *casus belli*. One day they will strike out and justify it easily if we don't match their ante. If good things are going to be done in response to the climate crisis, they'll probably be done for the wrong reasons, and it won't be in the sweeping way that is necessary for our long-term future.

Jeff Bridges' movie; 'Planet of the Humans', highlights this, in that brusque, Michael Moore, not-quite-right way. 'Twas poorly put together even if basically correct, and old anti-capitalist hippies have had their day already. The post-colonial world we live in is no longer conducive to worldwide changes in attitudes being fostered by the west, but we must affect one more in environmentalism. Europe and some other developed countries are the champions of climate change, which is rather unfortunate for the globe, given our history, and especially given the attitude of our dear leaders; the mighty United States of America; the most powerful country in the history of the Earth.

We are simply too comfortable with the festering open sore that is American leadership on the environment. The USA has usurped European power, but they have not led us; spiritually, economically or ideologically. Consider this; there isn't a single element of America's system of governance that we would have for ourselves. We would not have their education, their justice system, their politics, or their healthcare. We would not have their police, their military, or their civil authorities. We'd barely let them run a lemonade stand, being only good at making money, yet we rely on their defence of liberty, and their propagation of justice, while they commit global crimes in our name. All they have is the force of their military. The dollar only has value because there is a man with a machine gun who says it does. Only on one continent is the development of ideological and intellectual power moving in the right direction, after a great many horrific lessons learned. Europe will lead the next revolution as it has led the last few and possibly *because* it has led the last few, while our dear American leaders continue to dig for coal and engage in pointless wars to prop up their oil-soaked economy. And yet, who are we to once again foist our beliefs on a world long-tormented by Europe?

I do believe we need a <u>global</u> change in our ideology and beliefs. It is not enough to support a free-market economy coupled with democracy to deliver the best possible outcomes. It has only created prosperous economies and freedoms where education and development was already high. In order for democracy to work well, we must hope for an educated population, and for that education to be delivered in such a way as to foster progressive values that allow for change, especially since we need lots of change. The best education in the world cannot work against the fundamentals of religions that advocate the destruction of others. It's really no surprise the Arab spring led to such a disaster; the election of fundamentalists, military coups and widespread anarchy and brutality. Compare it to Ireland. It took nearly a century for us to shake off our catholic fundamentalism and evolve into the progressive socialist republic we first imagined.

In general, it has taken centuries of hardship and horror for Europe to become a place where freedom and equality are espoused and religious fundamentalism has been quashed. It is only recently that a few good democracies have really taken off. And it is to those few responsible governments that the whole world must turn in order to have any hope of harnessing the technological gains of the last few decades for good humanitarian uses. The technology we require in order to maintain our growth and development must be in the hands of responsible governments and organisations, and despite the rampant development of all the countries we once thought of as backward, I still only trust a handful of European powers, and a tiny cohort of non-European powers such as… Canada to exercise huge power responsibly. I struggled to come up with more than one. You can never negotiate with a tiger when your head is in its mouth. If Kim Jung Un were about to save the world, we'd stop him.

Although there is an explosion of technology and advancements that you might look to in order to save the world from environmental collapse, that technology is not only in the hands of responsible people. The advancements to fight climate change are largely in the hands of individuals and organisations such as universities and corporations. Small groups are experimenting with geo-engineering on a global scale without the global mandate required to exercise global changes. This is highly irresponsible. When new technology is put to use by well-meaning people in order to save the world, no one really has responsibility if it all goes wrong.

Some very promising technology for the production of clouds and for the whitening of clouds is being developed and deployed by a team of wealthy individuals whose reasoning is philanthropic, but whose oversight is nil. Their technology is being deployed whether we agree to it or not and the long-term effects are being gambled on without our consent. Who knows if spraying saltwater into clouds has dreadful effects if practiced for long enough, on a wide enough scale? Probably not, but we don't know for sure. A small group are doing it anyway and more power to them; they're trying to save the world from impending doom in the absence of governments trying to do the same. We need a lot more like them. However, if wealthy individuals can seek to affect the world for the global good, then equal opportunities exist for groups of individuals who seek to affect the world for nefarious reasons.

I've mentioned how any individual, such as myself, if given enough resources, could work to create chemical or genetic disturbances to the world on a grand scale. With our brilliant advances in medical technology comes the capacity for someone to abuse it. A few years ago, when Crispr technology grabbed headlines, the technology to cheaply alter DNA, I suddenly realised that if I wanted to I could pour millions of dollars into altering DNA and have devastating effects on the world, if only I had the millions to spare. I was thinking of making girls taller at the time, not taking over the world. People are seeking to create genetic mutations in mosquitoes that would render them infertile and thus stop the spread of blood-borne diseases, and if this idea is anything other than science fiction, then couldn't you equally imagine a horny man somewhere who thinks it would be great to wipe out the male population of his country in order to guarantee himself some female company? Or a berserk nationalist or fundamentalist who thinks it would be great to bring about some terrible genetic disaster on the population of Israel, or North Korea, or Ireland?

These are possibilities that have opened up in recent years, and I would be absolutely flabbergasted if there weren't some evil researchers somewhere working on some terrible virus or poison. Long have these kinds of dystopian evils been the remit of only the most powerful governments in the world, but now we have wealthy individuals whose organisations rival the largest economies on earth. Coca-Cola or Google would have just as much potential as Russia to go about researching some devastatingly evil genetic mutation. If you could make a mosquito who bit people and gave them a craving for Coca-Cola, or a cure for diabetes, then you might just become a trillionaire!

And it's not just corporate wealth that has the capacity to run research labs. Consider the wealth of lunatic groups such as scientology or other religions, and their reckless leadership. Consider the wealth of NGOs and charities. Consider the wealth of numerous departments that are outside the jurisdiction of their governments around the world, who perpetrate actions that are not mandated by their executive powers. (need I say more without disappearing in the middle of the night with a black sack over my head and end up in Guantanamo?) Consider the legacy wealth of families, clans and clubs around the world. The most dangerous groups these days are created and led by individuals who have accrued influence and power outside of governmental control, but with resources to expend nonetheless. Large tracts of the world are ungoverned, and large swathes of resource production and trading is uncontrolled and unaccounted for.

   The organisations who engage in crime are some of the biggest and richest in the world. We have an ever-increasing danger of technology falling into the wrong hands, quite apart from the headline-grabbing nukes everyone is afraid everyone else could get, even though the most dangerous countries have loads of them already. I'm much more concerned with the other technologies' ability to spread. We have watched as China laughed at our legal mumbo-jumbo and just ripped off everything the west invented, including our dangerous stuff like jets and rockets. They certainly have control over whatever biological weapons the yanks and bears made, in their wisdom. And who else can read about and develop their own genetic technology? If I can think it, anyone can. Someone will seek to do great harm; whether in the name of Yahweh or Allah or Mao, in the name of mine over yours, me over you, or this way over that way. I can't trust humanity too deeply.

   We fear war, with justification, but the current wars are not really wars in the way we would normally think of them. We still live with the threat of open conflict spilling out between countries, but it is a dwindling threat. The only wars between nations in recent times have been very asymmetric and ultimately irresolvable assertions of power by the US and co. The wars we see more widely are the campaigns being conducted by groups and militias without such centralized leadership. The reason for this is simple; we have a winner, but they haven't won. Since WW2, the USA has held the whole world in check, so it is absolutely pointless for anybody to fight them. They easily crush any country (without really winning) that doesn't conform to their world order, much like Britain did not so long ago, and they have enforced a change on the world, which for many, has been great. But they haven't beaten all the reasons that war has ever been fought for, which is why we still see countries fight America despite how futile and pyrrhic it is.

They've only won by threatening and inflicting devastation, not by removing the ideologies and differences for which war has always been fought. While there are wild differences in our ideologies and attitudes to each other, we will continue to have war. We cannot agree our purpose on this earth, much less the vacuous things, so we will fight to have our reasons win. And if that war cannot be fought openly without inviting a crushing destruction of whatever society America brings it to, then it will need to be fought by guerrillas and 'terrorists', all over the globe, wherever it can take root and have haven. It's sickening to say such inflammatory things, but we've lived through the truth of this, haven't we?

I hate the term terrorist, when really what we mean by it is religious fundamentalist. I don't hold that liberation warriors are necessarily terrorists, no matter where they're from. When they commit atrocities, they are criminals and monsters instead of terrorists, but I cannot condemn the cause of those **forced** to take up arms against unjust subjugation. And where they must take up arms, there must be blood. Obviously, it'd be better any other way. Unfortunately, the terms by which we understand liberation and justice have not been agreed. I cannot say it's wrong for an oppressed people to rise up against someone like Assad, for example, but if the people's idea of justice would be to then drive Assad's Alowite people into the sea for their crimes, or commit genocide on all other religious groups Assad protected, then I have a different conception of liberation and justice.

It's impossible to truly differentiate between

terrorist and freedom-fighter, because so much of our collective ideologies are based entirely on our own ethnic or religious group, at the expense of all others. No religion is innocent of this, of course. Perhaps some even espouse values of acceptance and tolerance, but even in those societies oppression is rife. Tibet was no utopia under the Dalai Lama. Go look it up. Religion is especially guilty of espousing intolerance, however nicely they dress it up, and ethnic and religious intolerance go hand in hand. The very act of being a proponent of one spiritual truth makes you a detractor to the others by default.

An ethnic group is literally defined by a perceived difference in culture and value; there is absolutely no scientific basis for race or ethnicity. It is an entirely human construct, like religion. It is entirely a belief, founded on nothing but a faith in our own culture and values. We are fundamentally riven by our 'beliefs' and we will never know true peace on earth until those beliefs align. If I were for one faith or another, I can see how it would be terribly tempting to say we need to usurp the authority of all other gods and have everyone follow THIS set of values and beliefs. But that's ugly and wrong.

Thankfully I'm of no religion. This will be hard for you to swallow, but it is the hard truth; belief in one ideology or another **_IS_** the downfall of humanity and the root of all evil. If you are a hard-core communist, or an outright fascist, or a bible-beater, we cannot peacefully coexist when the rational truth forces us to make decisions that fly against your dogma. The main conflict of the last century has been between those who reject any dogma, and those that cling to one, or another, or simply to their right to hang onto any at all. You can't. You must face up to the truth that reality presents. Communism doesn't work. There is no god. Black people just have ever-so-slightly more melanin in their skin. E=MC2. If we made decisions based only on demonstrable facts, we wouldn't have as much stupid war, I think. We might just have clever war instead. I think we're still just not quite done with war yet, unfortunately.

Many people don't see or appreciate the suffering of others, but it is there in wild abundance out there in the world and awareness of it hurts us and impacts our own wellbeing. There are brutal conflicts all around the place amongst other things. In my lifetime we have watched endless grisly conflicts unfold, terrible to be left without intervention, worse when we intervene. The increasing refugee crisis is merely a taste of things to come, rest unassured. We face one humanitarian crisis after another, and things have changed in the last century, as we've noted. We now have an organised conscious response to the movement of people and its causes more than any time in our past, but we have no convenient solution to the reality that people will be forced to migrate… forced to flee… without an end in sight, as they ever have. As the Irish have done for centuries.

If we do not seek to impose solutions globally, the wealthiest countries will ponder an ever-increasing conundrum. If we seek to impose solutions on the world, we will have war. There's no easy way out of further conflict. If we impose a hard-fought 'peace' on the whole world, who will make responsible governing decisions over that? Who is going to take global responsibility for the spending of our finite resources, and how will they do that? We need the world to begin to operate responsibly all together in the next decade to fight climate change. How can that need co-exist with the unresolved geopolitical conflicts everywhere? Have I said 'Fuck China' yet? Sorry to be guttural, but I cannot sufficiently express their evil, though I will continue to try. I have friends in concentration camps or dead as far as I can tell. Do you?

Ideally, we'd need to resolve all the world's differences over ideology without spilling a drop of blood, and agree to do the pragmatic thing environmentally, even while disagreeing about a bunch of other stuff, but I'm not terribly optimistic we'll be able to live a good long lifetime without at least one terrible global conflict. And if I can win that conflict by burning more coal and people than you, than I damn well will whatever the cost. We're just at the later stages of the first generation ever to go without a proper country-v-country world war on a grand scale. Will my generation be so lucky?

We still have a number of outstanding combatants who I don't entirely trust not to begin a world-ending conflict. Whether we look at the countries on top first, or all the countries from the bottom up, we are still in a delicate global balance, despite the apparent outright American dominance. There are plenty of countries who are on the verge of devastating conflict with one another, and have been for a while. As I write, we are imagining the Shia world uniting under Iran and having a brutal war with the yanks, Saudi's and Israelis, which the Hezbollah would of course lose, more-or-less. The Russians continue to flex their muscles in alarming ways. But there are others, and not even all conflicts necessarily including the yanks. What if Pakistan and India hurl nuclear missiles at each other? As absurd as it sounds, it may yet come to pass.

The problem once again is our hubris in trusting anything to have permanence, this time coupled with nukes and other dreadful weapons. We are probably at a stage now, thankfully, where even if there were open conflict between the USA and Russia, or India and Pakistan, it's hopefully unlikely they'd IMMEDIATELY nuke the world into Armageddon. I do not trust this to always be the case. How many presidents or leaders of all relevant countries are we likely to see in one lifetime? At least a particular one is just stupid enough to do something that would cause an all-out nuclear war. In any case, how long will it be before someone fires another nuclear missile or bomb in anger again on this planet? If the answer's not forever, that's not good enough.

Isn't it likely that wherever in the world a nuclear attack is carried out, there will be a very short window of time in which every nuclear-armed leader on earth will be contemplating their response? How much do you trust this assorted collection of villains and ne'er-do-wells to not retaliate or utilise that moment to use their own? We now laugh at the hysteria of people during the cold war, all the while living no further than a half hour from a nuclear war at any time ourselves. I know you will think this hysterical, thanks to the wonderful new paradigm we've fostered, but trust me. China hates the world. It would invade Japan, Taiwan and Korea immediately if the USA were otherwise engaged. They are very sore about what happened to them during WW2. Russia wants its USSR land back. Iran wants to be left al… oh… to create a Shia caliphate without freedom or tolerance, and wipe Israel off the face of the earth? Oh good. India and Pakistan want Kashmir. Ireland wants Ulster. Kim wants the South.

One opportunity will be everybody's opportunity. When the lid was rattling the pot before WW1, no one thought war would boil out. No one thinks the simmering tensions between Russia, Syria, Iran, China and USA could break out. Did anyone see the military exercise Russia, China and Iran did around the straits of Hormuz a few weeks ago? Is this pot-lid starting to rattle and whistle a little? I know this will now be old news to you, but at all times there are much higher moments of tension taking place than we are aware of. Military exercises never stop, though are rarely newsworthy. Trump might actually be right about one thing; the need for the other responsible powers to spend money on NATO and military. I know we don't like to think about a militarised Germany, but fuck me, they were good soldiers. And China has millions in its army. Tens of millions in reserve. They could potentially beat the USA single-handedly today, which is terrifying, and must never come to pass.

Long may we continue to live in the 'long peace' of Europe! I really hope we can hold it together peacefully because everyone wants to continue to do business. That line about doing business is our saving grace. Our greed is our saviour. As long as the world economy ticks along nicely and we can all continue to do business with each other then we should be ok. A cynic, who is also correct, will point out that all of America's conflict in the Middle East has been driven by their economic interest in the Saudi Kingdom and other oil-producing gulf states. The oil won't last though. The growth of these oil-rich nations is going to be a source of ongoing conflict and strife for generations to come. The USA won't be able to afford this global net of military for much longer either. At the very least, we can expect to see huge humanitarian problems as populations that have grown due to oil-wealth will suddenly realise their desert won't produce enough potatoes to feed themselves, and they'll flock to the fertile parts of the world. Or be driven there by their numerous enemies.

It's such an obvious source of future human migration, it's ludicrous. In the Emirates, they've literally built skyscrapers on sand, requiring the pumping of sand through the foundations to stay standing. The unsustainability of the cities of sand is glaringly obvious, and their spiritual architects are the most irresponsible people on earth. But then again, these Emirs are leaders bereft of any humanity; torturers, rapists, tyrants, paedophiles, bigamists and slavers. These are the people we must do business with, or face catastrophic global war, and will eventually have to rescue or abandon once the oil runs out. The host of the next world cup stand out especially; they're not even good at football, just purely corrupt.

It's a minuscule chance that the apocalypse I feel in my waters will be caused simply by a big war, but the tiny possibility leaves a fairly grim hope we'll be able to do the multitude things necessary to preserve nature and save the environment. And as our grinding progress brings more and more dangers to our attention, or forces us to take drastic action to remedy some contamination, the likelihood of geopolitical conflict is increased. What will we do about nations who refuse to act responsibly? Or nations that flip-flop between every election? How will we restrict the growth of populations in places where essential habitats are under threat? Sections of the world will be convinced of their moral duty to preserve some jungle or other habitat deemed essential, while others will advocate their full exploitation. The desire to constrain the population of any region will elicit their resentment.

By 2050 the population will have sailed past ten billion, despite the western optimism that suggests we'll squeeze just under. Every few years there is an update to the predicted population 'plateau'; it was predicted in my lifetime that the population would 'level out' or even shrink once it had reached 9 billion, then 10, now 11.5. The truth is this is more of a hope than a prediction, and we will likely go much further. Anything more than 2 children per 2 people will cause population to increase, and there are billions of people who could potentially be dutiful to their religious dogma. Some estimates see our populations' unhindered growth up to 20 billion. Unacceptable. It cannot come to pass.

The numbers are skewed by life-expectancy growth, certainly, I'll grant you. On the other hand, the plateau scenario is based on the belief that inequality will decrease and destitute nations will develop into wealthy ones, which for a number of reasons will not. I hope to live long enough to see, but dread seeing, 12 billion. When will too much become unacceptable? Already is undeniably the environmentally-correct answer; the evidence brooks no argument. We are five billion past sustainable. Then therefore, I am brought to the worst question of all. What if, despite all its horror and inhumanity, war is necessary in order to save

the world, or other terrible things? If we need to reduce
population and attempt to ensure that responsible governance
is in place to oversee the rationing and distribution of global
resources, then it may likely occur to someone somewhere
that they should be the ones to come out on top. Or that they
have the best reason, or the most powerful mandate, or the
greatest need.

The proper Machiavellian interpretation of our
paradigm is that the easiest path to saving the world from
humanity's malignancy is to conquer, control, and perhaps
eradicate opposition, because if you don't you will have
assured mutual destruction by competition. Therefore, many
will fight. Remember that breeding is a competition between
cultures and groups. We all wish to have our line extend
forever, to the extent that perhaps one day all humans will be
descended from us. That is our one imperative as living
things. We are almost the only species that ever chooses not to
reproduce. Someone will eventually realise that rather than
changing our lifestyles and brazen environmental disregard, a
simpler solution would be to kill billions and control the rest.
ISIS, essentially. Obviously I do not advocate this. We must
instead somehow convince everyone to do it together
voluntarily by stopping breeding, and not cheat.

Ultimately however, I do not trust you people.
We are all in a contest, even if you don't see it, participate
freely in it, or want it. You are bound towards a conflict of
interests as an intrinsic part of the nature of life. You need
resources. You will probably seek to reproduce. No nation
will limit their population while their neighbour doesn't, so
we will be forced to compete for dwindling resources. You
seek to incrementally accrue or inflict your influence on the
proceedings of the institutions and environment you are part
of. You wish to see your beliefs vindicated and your justice
recognised. If you don't, you are losing. We incrementally
change the zeitgeist around us intrinsically, even if all we do
is robot-walk around trying not to. Those who utilise their

influence have much more to say about how the future will be. Literally the clothes you choose to wear on a daily basis influence the multitudes who pass you in the street. I have already pointed this out, but you are individually incredibly more influential and important than you think.

The maths of our network of relationships shows us we are potentially four or five steps from communicating a thought or meme to almost every human on earth, except for Dave who lives in a cave, and the poor other Dave's and Davina's who live in prison-states; Belarus, north Korea, etc. However, we're in a competition of perspectives, values and beliefs that makes it difficult to seem like you're influential. Dominance is hard-fought. If you are going to be a sucker, and let some half-baked least-worst compromise between abler influencers come to pass without any dissent, then you lose. We in the secular countries are quickly becoming vacuous and hedonistic with technology, science, and rightful godlessness. Humanitarianism has been virtue-signalled into our widespread behaviour, not for any fundamental belief in humanity, but merely as an instinctive judgement of others' perceptions of ourselves. The spiritual void has not been meaningfully filled or relieved. Nothing is believable, and nothing has been fully explained, spiritually.

We are disconnected from deeper contemplation, or treat it as another enjoyable distraction among a tsunami of others. It seems almost as if we are abandoning hope in favour of gratification. Those who think they have overcome the debate about the profundity of nature by avoiding it are simply losing the contest. To abstain is not to oppose. There is a quickly spreading morass in the old West, and if you're not aware of it you're very cossetted or lucky. I feel it presents itself in an ever-increasing cultural vulgarity and vanity, and behavioural thuggery, but that may just be about where I live. I see it in our consumerism and greed. I see it in our political disintegration.

We are decreasingly likely to be able to bring a large enough number of people behind a single political party. More than a third of us don't even vote. Our ideology and partisanship is splintering, and our faith in any organisation is failing. We are also becoming increasingly individual, which is intellectually wonderful, but politically difficult. It would be impossible to have popular movements coalesce into a powerful long-term political entity, because the first contention that arises splits the party. Part of the reason for this is a total lack of overall ideological belief that can explain or justify positions changing or compromise being reached. We don't believe in anything. This is not necessarily a bad thing either. For at least a few glorious decades it looked as if the whole English-speaking world was ready to support moderation and compromise, and principles of 'right' and 'left' were being left behind. It briefly looked as if we were going to abandon all political dogmatism and engage in properly sensible, somewhat boring, discussions of the actual issues in the cold hard light of scientifically observed data. But no, those decades were really just the first years of our abandoning any ideology or idea about how the future should look.

As we've turned our back on ideology we've also turned our backs on politics, because almost none of us can tolerate the ability of a properly thinking politician to compromise on her own deeply held position. We're too obsessed with the individual cult of celebrity. There's little space for nuance. We are living in an age of intellectual stagnation, on a political, philosophical, and ideological level, which is ironically parallel to an age of flabbergasting technological and scientific enhancement and understanding. It seems impossible the two should co-exist, but the one makes the other all the worse. Ultimately, this dichotomy and paradox of wealthy cultures in the world is leading us to disaster. It doesn't take anyone being particularly stupid or evil for evil stupid things to happen, all it takes is a lack of attention or care, and there's so much to pay attention to. I once was the only one who could spot that a document being asked for in school by the local government was fundamentally racist because everyone was so well-meaning they thought it was ok. You cannot first ask me to fill in their ethnicity and then grade them even if there's a seemingly non-racist reason to do so. Education is colour-blind no matter what an ignorant parliamentarian thinks. We are blind to our own ignorance, and only through awareness of your own ignorance is any trace of wisdom achieved. You never truly stop being ignorant about all possible things, but you can try to be aware when you are.

Before I come to my dire prediction of what must be done, there is one more section about the end of the world to write, and I write this not for the excitement or immanency of their threat, but for their reality; their simple incontrovertible nature. This is important as it forms the basis for what should be our entire purpose of being, our *raison d'etre*. The last words in this chapter must again sum up the dire prognosis for human survival into the next century and the next; my grandchildren and their children's world.

We must do anything and everything to bring a peaceful settlement to world governance. The paradox of this is its contradiction; we must use terrible force to stop us having to use worse force later. We must intervene where it is right to do so, and once again, the only right thing to do in any given situation is the absolutely best and most efficient method of containing the environmental disaster. Is it more resource efficient to topple a dictatorship, or to commit genocide by embargo and blockade? Obviously one answer is preferable, and the other is correct. Which leads to healthier great-grandchildren? Who gets to decide?

Now you will recognize that I suffer from a severe lack of trust in my fellow man, but you needn't suffer under the same burden. If I remove myself and try to think objectively, it is clear that we are in fact much nicer than we imagine ourselves to be. In a real emergency, when it really hits the fan, we help each other. Despite what we see in some movies and TV shows, when things go terribly wrong the vast majority of human beings make tremendous sacrifices to assist one another. We never burst into rampant rape, pillage and murder as we often see in apocalyptic films. In fact, we almost mindlessly throw ourselves in harm's way to save each other. In the worst disasters around the world it is our humanity that triumphs. We simply need to harness that natural instinct for the greater good. The emergency approaching humanity is so big it is almost impossible to perceive without losing hope. But if we can awaken a deep realization right now, I objectively reason that the species called Homo-Sapient can pleasantly surprise even a pessimistic early-middle-aged misery-boots like me. The world hasn't ended yet.

There is still a shred of hope.

6: And just all the other natural normal stuff that can kill us all at any moment

Here's where you'll really start to really think of me as a crack-pot, but I don't care. The reason it's important to talk properly about the natural annihilations that can, and have occurred, is that it puts the final nail in the coffin of the question of whether we <u>should</u> think the world is really about to end. If you believe the world is likely about to end, then you are forced to think of solutions in advance of it physically taking place. If you don't believe in the man-made apocalypse, which is probably one or two lifetimes away at most, it doesn't matter. You would still surely want to protect yourself from non-manmade disaster, and some of the solutions are the same.

There are *deus ex-machina* events we know can befall earth, have befallen earth before, and that we can essentially only pray will not befall us. It feels like all we can do is trust that there is some reasonable purpose in our existence on a cosmological level that will hold back the extinction events that we have seen evidence of everywhere in our geological and archaeological past. To continue to live on this one planet is to hope that there is a divine intervention holding it together as a permanently ideal location for us to live. Unfortunately, that doesn't seem to be the case. We've just been lucky. There's a whole bunch of things that could obliterate us and every other living thing, in time periods from instantly to just slightly slower than instantly. If we're really serious about this whole 'life' business, then we can't afford to stand around arguing about saving it. We have to do anything we can conceive of, and do all of it now, in order to hedge our bets and really have any chance of preserving life. It's all that matters.

We are charged with the knowledge that if we were to strive together we could achieve a kind of immortality for living things by spreading them far and wide. Every one of us has imagined how our future space empire will look, but if it doesn't in the long run contain chimps and dolphins and gorillas and elephants and rhinos and lions and jaguars and penguins... we are a disgrace to mother nature, and contemptuous of the system that has propelled us into being. We can currently be reasonably sure we are the most intelligent and able species anywhere, and the living world around us is what has brought us about, and as we transcend it intellectually, we owe life a grave debt and still depend on life's resilience too. The following are five reasons why we are obligated to seek to colonise and create new habitats for life to thrive in, wherever that may prudently be, and to develop the means to live sustainably and spread our wealth more evenly whatever the cost and discomfort.

Solar flares and Coronal mass ejections

Very often, the boiling seething mass of the sun shoots out massive flares of material and energy caused by explosions under the surface, from seemingly random points all around its globe. These flares punch far out into space, and occasionally we get licked by them. You can think of it as solar weather in the radiation emanating from our great host. Its fluctuations cause the aurora. In our age of technology, we have not really suffered an extreme storm striking us directly, but we've had a few localised events, like the Canadian event in 1989.

Recently, my brother and fellow author Conor wrote a paper about the economic impact of a solar flare on Australia, considering the more common kind up to the bigger kinds. It would be very costly, needless to say, given the scale of their electrical infrastructure. If a solar storm on the scale of the one in 1859 were to hit the earth right now, the effects on our economy and infrastructure would be devastating. But there are even bigger ejections possible. In 2012, we were missed by a whisker by a coronal mass ejection and solar flare that would have disintegrated half the world's electrical capacity. This happens because the solar particles hit the earth with such force they ionize the atmosphere filling it with energetic electrons that would destroy all our electronic devices and infrastructure. Basically imagine a blanket of weak lightning falling on every point and frying anything conductive. We got real lucky.

It's only a matter of time before we are hit again in a significant way, and if we are hit directly by some of the biggest possible ejections we'd be getting a fairly significant dose of radiation ourselves. It all depends on how it hits us and how big the ejection is, but if the most productive industrial regions of earth were struck heavily, it would take a long time and stupendous cost to recover. Our civilization has become dependent on the technology we've developed between solar storms, so we are extremely vulnerable to the effects of an inevitable danger. We have to hope that there is divine intervention on the roulette table that prevents our sector ever getting its share until we are ready to cope with it.

We'd be much more prepared to deal with this problem if there wasn't so much inequality on earth. The fact that manufacture and development is concentrated leaves the whole world in danger. To prevent this danger from radically affecting our way of life in any one lifetime we must spread our wealth and development far and wide. If we had manufacture and resources equally divided around the globe and off the globe, we could quickly recover from any partial destruction of electrical and manufacturing infrastructure. But if Europe were widely affected, the world economy would tumble. If the USA were badly affected, all hell would break loose.

Cosmic outbursts

It's not just the sun that can bathe us in deadly particles and energy. At any moment, any quasar or supernova could have us in its sights. A quasar creates a Jetstream of material that would instantly obliterate us and is literally astronomically improbable, but there's nothing preventing a binary star system in our neck of the woods from causing a supernova type outburst of particles and gamma radiation. As soon as we see the light of the event happening we will be feeling its cosmic rays. Even though Betelgeuse is a good distance away, if it were to explode, which it may shortly, it would be very bright in the sky at night for a while, perhaps bright enough to see in the day. Most star systems are binary star systems like Betelgeuse and these systems are much more likely to cause supernovas and gamma ray bursts as stars are torn apart by gravitational forces when a big star orbits a dense star, typically, or when there is a new gravitational interaction with another system. Suns literally explode in their interactions with one another quite often.

As our understanding develops it seems increasingly unlikely that life could exist further into the centre of the galaxy due to the increased density of star systems and the dynamic storms of energy forces and particles. We live in more than one 'goldilocks' zone of habitability living out on one of the arms of the outside of the galaxy, but we are not immune to random events of a cosmic nature just blinking life out on earth at any moment. The moment we see it happening, it will whip away our magnetic shield and bombard our atmosphere, possibly causing it to be catastrophically reduced and irradiated and heated. I don't know whether we'd boil or asphyxiate first.

There is nothing to be done but hold on to our

hats and hope for the best, and do everything we can to make life a multi-planetary endeavour, or think about space colonies. We must continue and hasten the search for life in space, because a very big question in how we plan to develop going forward hinges on the probability of life. Either we find life pretty much everywhere it can be all around the solar system at least at a microbial level, or we find the universe miraculously sterile, inviting its own question about the viability of life at all, for precisely this reason. If there is life it might be difficult for us to spread to other planets and utilise the materials of space, so we'll need to have orbital habitats and industrialisation, or figure out drastic ways not to cross-contaminate and introduce dangerous unknowns to life on planets and moons and ourselves.

If there isn't any life out there, which would blow my mind and make me think up a god, then our job of ensuring life can go on is incredibly easy. We can seed life wherever we foresee its propagation. A lack of life would be some unbelievably lucky opportunity to take over the universe, and a very scary warning about the dangers to life on a cosmic level. If there isn't even microbial life out there at least in one or two other places in the solar system, you can be sure that it's just too hard for nature alone. We are some kind of stupendously improbable miracle. But don't get carried away. Occam's razor. There will probably be loads of life, possibly all very different too, and that will be a challenge for humanity's survival also. This seems most likely.

Asteroids/etc.

This is an exceptionally unlikely extinction level event to happen in any one lifetime, I grant you, but it is still an ever present danger. From the very tiny objects to the ones the size of a couple of buses that can only do a little bit of damage, we have no notice of their coming at all. Most of the bigger near-earth objects are being tracked, and a colossal amount have been found, so it does seem increasingly unlikely a local object has our name on it. However, the rare wild-card comets and interstellar objects of any size that are out there will not necessarily be known to us except by chance. We will possibly get a couple of months warning that an object has been detected with a high probability of impact, if it is a large and energetic enough object to be profoundly destructive.

It may be many lifetimes before such an event comes to pass, but as can be seen by all the craters everywhere, the universe is a busy place geologically. If a large space object hits a continent, you can be pretty sure that continent will be uninhabitable for a while, and the rest of the world would suffer a nearly completely devastating fall-out. If such an object hit an ocean, the tidal waves could circle the globe. There are countless near-infinite objects falling around between the sizes of 2 miles wide to 60 miles wide. A two-mile-wide thing would be devastating but life would go on, in whatever harsh dystopian cave-man way that it does. One at the top end of the spectrum, a 60-mile-wide rock would essentially turn the entire crust of earth into a hellish ash and lava filled death spiral that would very quickly eradicate all life completely. Almost instantly, but just horrifically not quite. You might be aware and awake as the ground turns to lava.

Obviously we must continue to keep an eye out, and invest in bigger and better telescopes and satellites and detection technology, but we also need to be ready to do something about it at a moment's notice. I'm not certain what that something exactly is yet, but I'm sure there are some cool people cooking up potential solutions somewhere. Just knowing that it's even possible, however incredibly improbable it is in a short space of time, should be enough prompt to realise we need to be making moves to mitigate or prevent it immediately, while we still can.

Of course it will probably take the rest of my

lifetime for the species to take serious collective effort on this issue, but I would be seriously surprised if we will not have the capacity to avoid an asteroid impact, no matter how sure we are there are none out there to get us. We will also always be peppered by the smaller ones, and sure as day follows night, one will eventually hit a city of consequence and cause a huge cost to the environment and economy. So I'm certain we will collectively seek to spread ourselves out into space and build the necessary infrastructure and readiness to always seek to avoid any damage befalling earth at all. Surely, won't we?

<u>Volcanoes</u>

So let's talk about the Permian extinction folks. We cannot really predict when a super-volcano will go off. The Permian extinction that led to the following age of dinosaurs, was an incredibly destructive and devastating extinction event. The whole planet's vast array of land diversity was whittled down to only a few scant species who managed somehow to scrape their way through. It wasn't even as if the volcanoes that caused this extinction were one of the biggest and most dangerous types either. The Siberian traps simply spewed a very strong and steady plume of lava out for a very long time until a very large chunk of the earth was just lava, burying and disintegrating all life on a significant proportion of the globe.

The rest suffered from the noxious gases from the eruption and the fires it caused everywhere, probably bringing global permanent winter year after year, for thousands of years. Thousands of years!! A volcano could go off tomorrow and spew it's load for thousands of years!!! But there are even bigger scarier volcanoes. Yellowstone is a massive caldera for one of the biggest potential volcanoes on earth. There are several potential super-volcano sites, but none are more likely to blow than Yellowstone. It would be as devastating as a 2-mile-wide asteroid striking North America. The whole continent would be quickly uninhabitable and it would be decades from the end of the eruption to the end of the disruption and famine caused by the ash and material released into the atmosphere. We will get no notice at all, as far as I currently understand our capabilities. This could happen tomorrow. Yellowstone is looking unstable.

Once again it's obvious to say that we cannot be completely dependent on this one rock in the sky forever. We have been granted a miraculous window in time when we may become the kind of thing that seems to be so glaringly missing from the universe; a civilisation of space. Some of the greatest things we have ever achieved are the many robots out there orbiting around us or the sun, or on the surfaces of objects and moons and planets around the system. Perhaps our greatest two achievements are the two probes on their way out of the system to orbit the galactic centre, and the more we will send out there. These objects seem very likely to outlive our civilisation, which is glorious. And disquieting.

The universe seems to be governed by very deterministic laws and rules that seem to evolve chaotically, but we have free will and agency. We have the capacity to decide to change the course and purpose of objects and materials out in the ether, and harness them for our own enrichment and the furthering of our goals and aims. We must strive to do so or we will be at the mercy of the very thing we should be exploiting; the stupendous wealth of material and potential for expansion in space. We as a species have not reached mature adulthood until we have taken out an insurance policy of some kind or another.

The Fermi-paradox problem (possibly death aliens)

The Fermi paradox is a simple question; If the universe is so big and old, where are all the alien civilisations? Even though you might consider the pursuit of intelligent alien life to be the realm of conspiracy theorists and tin-foil hats, it is actually a focus of a large part of our real scientific endeavours. We are scouring the universe for any discernible sign of life or intelligence. There are whole branches of academia dedicated to the study of life in space. And all this is because it really matters. From the simple functionality of our attempts to spread out into space, to the pragmatism and viability of life itself, the question of 'where are all the aliens' has incredibly profound meaning for the future of earth and all its life.

There is some possibility we simply just can't see them yet, but all the other explanations to answer the paradox are dark potential problems that prevent life from gaining a substantial foothold in the stars, and we call these problems the 'great filters'. There is a lot of debate about which 'great filter' is most likely the reason the galaxy is empty. If it is one of the hurdles we have already overcome as a collective enterprise of life such as simply becoming multi-cellular, or crawling out of the sea, or not tearing ourselves apart in a brutal nuclear war, then hooray! But it seems likely the great filter may just as easily be ahead of us, given the criticality of a lot of the other things we've noted in this book, and the achingly lonely emptiness of our universe.

In this galaxy, the number of stars is larger than our relative experience will allow us to comprehend; somewhere between 150 and 250 billion. The number of galaxies in the observable universe is beyond incomprehensible, again hundreds of billions, each containing their own indigestible number of stars. And as we rapidly expand our search through the universe for meaning, we find that almost every star is host to its own collection of planets and debris. The probability that other planets exist out there with all the advantages of earth is certain. There is a principle in science that is generally found to be true, that if only one example of a specimen or phenomenon is observed, then it is most likely to be closer to average and typical, than it is to outrageously rare and extreme. There simply must be other intelligent civilisations out there in the universe, and the capacity for them to exist has been around for billions of years. There should not only be civilizations, but extravagantly advanced civilizations. And millions of them. And so far we see not one jot of evidence for it.

That raises a question of likelihoods. Which is more likely; that we are trend-setters and may therefore conquer the whole galaxy, or that there is something that prevents any civilization from reaching a level where their existence would be forever obvious to any other in the galaxy? It seems likely that if we continue towards optimistic projections of our advancement, we are only a few hundred years from leaving an indelible and unmistakable stamp on the galaxy. We must desperately seek an answer to the fermi paradox in that time, whether it is because of some natural flaw in space-faring life's viability, or some great filter like self-destruction, natural destruction or unnatural destruction at the hands of some entity yet to be identified. What if there's something out there that somehow stifles intelligent advancement? It's more likely to be the harsh environments we encounter than some alien or AI overlord, but there certainly seems to be something holding back the development of interplanetary empires out there which is not entirely clear. Is it all just a simulation? Then what do we have to do to win the game? Something is simply not right out there.

7: What needs to be done

It has been a while between writing that chunk of the book and writing this. I have basically pondered the very question I'm about to explore my entire life. It's tricky. I have many drafts, all just that bit more palatable than this, but none as true or heartfelt. What are we meant to do? What is the bloody meaning of it all? What's the question that will give us forty-two? How best to exercise this mammoth power of free will and influence? How do we prevent our imminent collapse?

Finally, I think I have identified a meaning to human life. That is a daring claim. It is not a charming or gratifying meaning, just a profoundly important and true meaning. I will spell it out soon. Be patient; it's very simple. I have researched and written and explored every nice possible way I could imagine to bring us towards a future worth living in, but it doesn't seem to exist, at least not without stupendous advancements and cost. I do hope for the advancements, but there needs to be a faster and more secure way of protecting the future life of this planet and this species. I cannot see how else we will survive in a tolerable way… let's say 40 years into the future. I am young! Will we last long enough for fusion to solve our problems? With enough power you could do anything.

I have written a play where a 20,000-year-old man meets a modern man after an alien abduction and they explore the ways in which humanity needs to develop, some of the problems and possibilities and desires that are universally human, and what it means to be alive. Naturally, it's a poor play with men, but I have grappled with my political and spiritual attitude all my adolescent and adult life, as a man. I have grown up with sci-fi books, TV and film that explore all the exciting things we can hope to achieve in the future, and have always wondered and speculated about what the future will look like; it's such an exciting time to be alive. And by goodness, how we've progressed in my lifetime. Never before have we been so tolerant and open and democratic and egalitarian, even if there are flaws in our politics. But the problem is, ultimately, the very real possibility that all our good intentions are extremely misplaced, and that the idea of our best governance being the most humanely caring one is wrong. With a sense of sad resignation, I have decided that it is no longer good enough, or fit for purpose.

Our current valuation and regard for individual freedom and wellbeing is ideologically flimsy in its purpose and places far too great a weight on human happiness at the cost of all else. The only evidence I can propose to convince you of this is the section of this book you've read by this point. But if you look into everything I have outlined; 25 ways the world is about to end, as I first conceived of this book, you will discover for yourself the continually reactionary failure to govern which has been the defining feature of western democratic adventures since world war 2. We have left the world in a worse state than before, at the expense of improving our quality of individual lives and multiplying exponentially. We're not special enough, nor ever have been, to justify the evil that has been done to bring us here, in so many fields of life and institutions, and in so many ways. My heart is drowning in disillusionment. I lay, with good evidence, almost all social strife and lack of cohesion in the world at the feet of ideological and spiritual disillusionment and the conflict between the two. We need a bigger purpose.

Those who lead and govern this world are not just the leaders of humanity, they are the leaders and keepers of all known living things in the universe. The arithmetic of human governance can no longer depend simply upon the wellbeing and prosperity of as many people as possible. It must enter all of the global biome's resources and creatures into account all at once, and act to aggressively address human dominance and waste. We must, as soon as we become national leaders, shed our humanity and act for the good of the earth and its inhabitants, rather than the paltry few thousands of electors who bothered to put you in office. They say the interests of the many outweigh the few, but the interests of the multitude obliterate the interests of the many. I say this because we must sadly abandon our growing sense of global fraternity, in favour of love for our natural world at the expense of human gains.

It is right and proper, and simply scientifically true, that we should abandon our racism and tribalism and hatred based belief systems, and that those conflicts are absurd and counter-constructive for the purposes of humanity's survival. But that is not to say that any and all people everywhere should be allowed to live and reproduce in absolute freedom, and that we should never have conflict again. Potentially our evolutionary history has been preparing us for conflict all along. We must limit the growth of the population. We have already gone way too far beyond our capacity to cope with long term, and we have a choice between imposed limitations and natural limitations. Natural boundaries will be discovered through mass starvation and famine only. I would rather fight wars to impose sterilisation than to watch those burgeoning semi-industrialised countries implode in dreadful famine. And that, unfortunately is what will probably have to be done in the long run. I know it is dreadful to suggest there will be an unfair share of the suffering in the developing world, but it is what we have seen, are seeing and will continue to see. The most urgent need for development and promotion of better and less impactful lives is in the third world despite our shameful wastefulness in the rich world. Good sustainability should see a reduction in our quality of life in the West until such a time that global quality of life is as close to equal as possible. I suspect it will always be nicer in my village than yours, however.

There are many other more pressing matters to attend to in the short term. The point of the example is there will be a great deal of ugliness or swiftness that will NEED to be perpetrated for the best and most enjoyable future for our children and grandchildren. It is not ok for everyone's children to have a fractional share of the future when we can decide for ourselves to enrich them, by giving them a larger fraction of all available resources in a controlled manner by simply shrinking the population. It is the old Irish problem of farmers dividing fields between his sons 'til there's more fence than field. We will not be able to continue to share the resources of the world indefinitely. Not even for very long. Obviously this easiest of solutions; population control, is the best way to save the future, but it is far-fetched. It is action that should be taken and won't. We will be greedy and selfish until the end I suspect.

However, I have several specific ideas and proposals for immediate action that should and must be taken, but before I come to those I must outline the overall tenet of my argument, and that is; we must become absolutely militantly environmentalist. We have to take very large scale drastic actions, with the more willing participants, the less suffering for all, but fewer willing participants, the more ugliness and cruelty. We will have to take people with us whether they like it or not. We will have to cook up the quickest and surest tactics for the protection of this planet, and potentially take those actions into our own hands. In order to achieve such goals, we must organise ourselves on a grand scale. Many will quickly beat their hooves to social media platforms, and that's fine, but that is unacceptable long term to anyone who accepts the reality of the situation. We must act to forsake a great deal of the modern comforts in order to guarantee the future. Yes, we should use the tools that are open and available, but we should not champion them, for their wasteful expenditure of resources. When your phone inevitably goes obsolete next week, please don't buy a brand new one.

For this to work it needs to be bigger than any mere social media event can muster anyway. It needs to be real. We need to meet as real people, on foot, wearing the heart and truth of what we believe on our sleeves for all to see. It is almost meaningless for one person alone to forgo the pleasure of a chemically-driven sweat-shop dependent garment industry, but if together on the streets we all do it for real, with our actions and not just our simulacra, then it has real power and real meaning. We have to start shaking ourselves out of our comfortable hedonistic lives for a few hours every day and go out and get things done. Find people. Find causes. Read. Research. Realise the extent of your influence and impact. Ask people uncomfortable questions. Where was the oil pumped that went into your lovely dress? Do you really think Mcdonalds is the best choice of food for your children today? Spare a carbon credit, sire? What will our grandchildren eat? Will humanity wake up when it's too late?

I have said I have deduced a meaning for humanity and it is simple. We have a mission that appears to be as close to god-given as we can scientifically discern; to protect and promote the life on this planet, and to help it transcend this world. We know this now scientifically, as well as through many spiritual traditions of the world. We need to become the gods we imagined for ourselves in our relationship to the other denizens of this beautiful planet. We must do anything and everything to protect and even nourish the natural world around us. We must tear down everything for a new purpose that is all-pervasive. We must extend the reach of our species. Imagine how far into the universe we would be now if all the resources, energy and manpower we have spent on the military in the last century had been directed towards space travel. Imagine a world where before world war 1 we had discovered an asteroid due to hit us within a hundred years. We would have conquered the solar system and vaporised that asteroid by now, instead of murdering each other by the millions.

It is preposterous that normal daily life should be allowed to continue in its endless meaningless triviality any longer. All human beings must be bent to the will and purpose of one all-inclusive purpose. War-time mentality. But this is like a real holy war, where the crusade is against ourselves as well as the heathens, and the god has been replaced with scientific methodology and an ongoing change, and potentially the new god of progress and human stewardship. Human wellbeing is a lovely tangent from the **real** purpose of our lives here in this universe.

There is an intolerable phrase often used; "We're here for a good time, not for a long time." WRONG! We are here for a short time, not for a good time. Hedonism has crept in and we no longer value the necessity for human suffering in order for there to be enjoyment of human achievement. Audrey Hepburn said "To be happy is the most important thing. It's all that matters." Oh yeah? Go take heroin, smoke crack and take LSD, then get back to me Audrey; drugs grant instantaneous happiness at the loss of all sensibility. I'd recommend tying LSD once for the profundity of the experience. It will make you stupendously happy momentarily. However, happiness is not the meaning of life; it is a lovely by-product of actually having a meaning in life. Nobody is envious of a junkie. Those who have everything lack the most important thing; the hope and desire for more and better things, and the drive to improve. Happiness comes after blood, sweat and tears. I think Audrey probably understood that, but many people who use her quote don't.

So what does this mean? What do we do? I think it should be very simple. We have quibbled like children over gimmicky political nonsense for long enough, and it is time to simply join up for one good reasonable purpose. We're still voting for the two sides in the civil war a hundred years ago in Ireland. Vote green! I think the ideal thing to do would be simply to go to the streets in the beginning. If you go to your high street and wait there, others will come. We should use every tool, but we should mostly use ourselves. I think that due to the extremely volatile nature of the actions I would condone us to do when organised, we wouldn't want to keep records of how we organised what needs to be done, so it's better to meet in person anyway. Give me fifty angry young adults, and a lever big enough, and I will change the world. But let's not be arrested immediately methinks.

There needs to be a new political and green force everywhere. I have lived all over the world and would hope that different people in different places all around the world would reach the same logical conclusions. We need to politicise and we need to organise. At first, the primary directive of this new green movement should be in peaceful protest and gathering, and minor acts of dissent, but I think from the very start, everyone needs to be prepared to go a long way further than 'Extinction Rebellion' went in the pursuit of particular goals. And stop giving things gimmicky names and memes like that! The imperative is far too important to try to be fun and lovely and paint the world in rainbows and unicorns. Extinction is fairly succinct, but it's not about the memes. They at least showed there is a generation of people acutely aware of the problem. They will only get angrier. They will soon be seething.

In Ireland in particular, but everywhere else too, an urgent and necessary action is the immediate closure of all coal, gas, wood and turf burning electrical production. We are literally burning the earth lads. I would suggest that the nice way to achieve this would be to have everyone turn off their lights and disconnect their houses until the government took action. This could take years. On the other hand, a few dozen determined eco-warriors could achieve this temporarily overnight. The cost in human suffering and economic loss is irrelevant. There will be criticism from all sides, though irrelevant and wrong. Economic loss is meaningless. I will brook no argument of financial or humanitarian origin. That is irrelevant.

This will be the crux of the opposition to this movement, and it will be exceedingly difficult not to brood over doubts and be talked down by reasonable, caring people. But let me steel your nerve a little. How do you weigh up the inconvenience and losses of drastic action now against the damned end of the world? It's not a conspiracy or a dream, but a reality hurtling towards us. We must stop the wastage of our world instead of standing around saying 'tsk tsk'. One simple action that I'm astounded isn't being taken is the dismantling of all street lights and other lights that are pissing our resources away every night in every city in every country of the world. It's thought a telescope from our nearest star would be able to detect our night-side electrical light; our light pollution is astronomically detectable. If local governments won't dismantle public lighting, we should do it ourselves. And hopefully recycle it somehow. There is very little need for it, beyond the fact that humans just need to be a little bloody nicer to each other at night-time.

I suggest we form lots and lots of groups determined to wreak havoc if we can't just win politically, but I don't propose a secret society of anarchists. The exact opposite in fact. I suggest that it be a revolution hidden in plain sight as an absolutely open and ongoing meeting of minds on the high streets of our towns. We will know each other in our clothes and our means of purveyance. We will not burn oil to come there or dress for a fashion parade on the backs of child labour in Bangladesh. We will not use destructive devices and resources to participate in this, even if we need to for other things. It must become such a feature of our lives to participate in this ongoing discussion and meeting, that it replaces our lives. Let's show the hippy generation what love and dedication really look like.

We should create the Forum on our streets as an ongoing development of our collective will. We must do this because it is the only environmentally sustainable and purely incorruptible form of collectivism; nothing else comes close. Many different ideologies and parties have tried ways to govern, but we need only simple principals to govern an anarchy of environmental action. All that is done must strive to change the future environment for the better and to further our goals to preserve this species and its life. A kind of anarchy within the institutional confines of our great nations. I wouldn't suggest committing really grave crimes, but in about a decade… sign me up for anything; I will fight tooth and nail. We have to act now, or it will be unforgiveable later. You younger than me will probably meet your grandson who starves in the coming global famine, or your great-grandson who asphyxiates next century. Think on that.

A major strand of this movement must of course be a completely un-negotiated acceptance of the goals of the overall mission. You must abandon your gods and your ideas of cultural propriety at the door. There is no time for delay while we mitigate for the poor circumstances of this group while worrying about that group. I don't want to meditate on the end of the world, I want to stop it. Our responsibility is to the greater whole and not at all to the individuals. If there is something we must or must not eat or consume or do for the greater good, then no instruction written in a thousand-year-old book has any merit in the face of scientific truth. We must stop multiplying, as god instructed. There must be a great deal of seemingly wrong and sinful lengths we must be ready to go to in pursuit of these goals if the urgency is not heeded in very short order. I'd like to emphasize that there still is time for reason and logic to win out peacefully, but that time is rapidly passing, and we must prepare and arm ourselves. Metaphorically and truly.

Potentially in the long run, I could see and justify and condone things like coups and the hostage-taking of governments in pursuit of environmental goals. I would be happy for wars to be fought in order to protect species and biomes from governments who don't fall in line with our environmental necessity. I would rather see countries tear themselves apart in civil wars than to continue brazenly to eradicate the life in their borders and pump their noxious pollutants out into the world without challenge. I feel quite justified in saying that if those royal Saudi monsters don't stop pumping oil in the next decade, we should go into their desert and stop them, whatever the cost. You might find 'monster' a little strong, but you don't know the language people use who really know them. Just read some of the leaked diplomatic documents from over the years. Our diplomats call them worse. Our diplomats. And one of the many reasons is this; the past king of Saudi Arabia passed in his nineties as a syphilitic paedophile with a child bride among his harem, with sons who have tortured and hunted human beings for sport. And that one family rule a subcontinent as their personal fiefdom and destabilise the whole region; one family. And yet still their worst crime is against the environment.

There is no redemption for those who continue to wilfully destroy the world. If Donald Trump cannot be shown, potentially with a colouring book, that he needs to stop being on the wrong side of this, then I would happily condone his impeachment by any means, if it weren't for the even more evil stupid bastard that stands behind him. I desperately hope Joe Biden can just oust him peacefully, but it is rigged against him, mark this word; gerrymandering. Unless he rides a landslide. American democracy is broken. Trump is the obvious 'exhibit A', but there are many more problems with it. It must be fixed immediately, but it won't be. This is not the time for patience. It is the time for extreme action and ultimatums. We're too close to Armageddon and Ragnarok and whatever other fairy-tale you imagine the coming starvation and asphyxiation to be.

It's getting a bit too late to be nice about any of this anymore. We live in an absurd time when all the 'richest' countries on earth are drastically and deeply in debt, living on borrowed time, and squabble over the most meaningless of trivialities, like money-making. Every country is in many times more debt than the debt we attempted to address in Live-Aid. No one will be able to eat money to survive when the famine comes anyway. No one has the slightest intention of ever repaying their debts to the world either. I suspect many world leaders know all this.

We do not visibly see it or speak of it publicly, but we live in an extremely precarious time politically around the world, and leaders everywhere are hoping for miraculous new developments and advancements to save their skin, while they double down (again lacking the correct order of magnitude) on destruction and greed, with grand giveaway elections, and the satiation of mere human needs and desires, with no overriding ideology whatsoever. It should no longer be the remit of the government of any sensible people to worry only about the happiness and wellbeing of its citizens. Their only duty is to Gaia, and to our gene-pool. Forget socialism. People are not worth it individually. Only collectively, and in our achievements do we have much value at all. I'm on board with all kinds of nationalization however.

In the short term, in a democratic country like Ireland, there are a number of simple goals that should be set out. It would be simpler and easier to take control politically through democracy, but I don't trust people. So, in the short term, the government should be forced to shut down any and all unacceptable environmental practices, closing down airlines and fossil fuel companies immediately and taking into national control all mineral and natural resources of the land,

by any means necessary. Any means necessary. All contracts
and uses of resources should be vetted for whether it matches
up with the long term goal of the people, which is to survive
long into the future. In Ireland that is already pretty much my
understanding of the constitution anyway. Certainly of our
declaration of independence from the UK.

It is completely and utterly meaningless how
many people have to go without electricity or cars for how
long or what the economic impact will be. That is utterly
irrelevant. The scale of the crisis we are trying to avert trumps
any moderating considerations and mitigating circumstances.
You might just about justify running a generator or two for a
hospital, but better yet if you can get 500 prisoners on
treadmills. There can be very little compromise due to human
happiness and suffering. The suffering of people now cannot
be compared with the immeasurable suffering of people yet to
come if we don't take these actions. I would rather suffer now
than see your children suffer more later, it's as simple as that. I
think every decent human being should feel the same and be
willing to sacrifice something for the future

There must also be an immediate end to all
relationships and trading with governments whose policies
and procedures are unacceptable, from Saudi Arabia to China.
It is disgusting that we allow those countries to treat their
people and land in such a way for our gratification. When I
was a teenager in China, I cycled over the crest of a desert and
saw a landfill filling the horizon, being picked over by
thousands of women and children, and it wasn't the Chinese
government who are to blame, entirely. It is us in the West,
who allow our 'recycling' and rubbish to be transported all
around the world. It was European rubbish. British rubbish.
We must stop all trade practices that we know are destroying
the earth. Substances such as palm oil and soya from Brazil
should be banned. Anything grown which we know is
choking the world must be banned immediately, like wood-
pellet forestry as another insane example of the false 'green'

narrative of oil companies.

We must tear down the false narratives of 'off-setting' and carbon neutralisation. No amount of offsetting forgives the burning of turf and coal and oil. You cannot offset a murder by raping and impregnating a woman, which is exactly what oil companies who invest in woodchip-burning for carbon credits are doing; offsetting murder with rape, and getting paid to do it. Growing trees to burn captures zero carbon. In energy-efficiency it is in fact worse than burning fossil fuel for carbon-per-megawatt. We need to take an extremely hard stance against multinational companies whose treatment of the global resources has been utterly irresponsible and downright evil in many cases. How much land is wasted growing bloody tobacco? How many people have starved because of Coca-Cola's handling of national water supplies? Why have they bloody well got national water supplies!?

The only sense in which the term offsetting has any relevance is in terms of households and individuals. It is right and proper that you personally and as a family try to balance your consumption with your contribution. If you must use something very damaging for large parts of the day for economic or other reasons, then you damn well better have a carbon-neutral house and grow your own spuds. We can calculate a ledger of carbon footprints for ourselves and other individuals and households and utilize this effectively to improve the world and we should be rewarded for doing so; in fact, it offers an amazing way of utilizing unemployment for environmentalism. If you can calculate a net contribution in your actions, then we could subsidize people to be self-reliant. Over time the poorest could actually accumulate wealth. However, rewarding any company or organization bigger than a family is an invitation to disaster. It is ridiculous for an airline to claim offsetting of their fuel consumption by planting trees in commercial forestry investments. This is a scam. A fifty-year transition from carbon is a very short-sighted scam, as it will kill us all inevitably. We have ten years at most.

It is not good enough to continue with this slow progressive transitional phase we're in now. The problem is the best wishes here in Ireland or in the UK makes not a damn bit of difference to how much is being burned at the other side of the world in case we MIGHT want their products. NO! We must attack and kill any and all practices that are unacceptable. A government like Ireland's should take a renegade position and demand the world catch up, because it's all we have the power to do. If I could get my hands on a few hundred thousand American soldiers though, and bring that country's brilliant industriousness to bear on the problem, the outcomes could be fantastic; the world could be changed overnight.

Now this is only if we can't get the right people elected soon around the world, but I think it may well then be time to momentarily shelve the wonderful dream that is democracy once more, for there is still a hard road to go and hard men and women will be needed. I could justify and condone a tremendous amount of civil dissent and outright revolution in the USA, because I cannot for the life of me imagine for one second a way in which that industrial goliath is going to be chopped down and rebuilt without oil and coal and gas and burning forests. The worst victim of the approaching end of resources will be the poor yanks, so I hope they grow some brains before the next election.

I've said a couple of times about coups etc. and you might think it's a bit evil, but I think there are ways and means it could be achieved with a minimal of bloodshed, and recent forms of action have been childish, if nice and peaceful, and mostly because the American democratic system is broken. In the end, the key to any extreme endeavour of that kind remaining incorruptible would simply be for the coup to relinquish power immediately when a particular thing has been done. For example, you could seize control for a few days, bulldoze the electricity plants to the ground and then surrender your arms and people. Then you stage a minor coup to free them if the judiciary is unjust and locks them up for serving the objectively correct greater good.

You might have a vicious cycle of violence, but no revolution lived without fighting for its comrades. People who stand up for what is right and good in this world should be applauded and revered instead of vilified like Edward Snowden, Chelsea Manning and Julian Assange. These three revealed despicable evils being perpetrated. Their captivity should be met with open revolt. Again this seems extreme, but I don't have time and patience to wait for slow old dickheads, whose generation is ruining the world, to come to the realisation that natural justice is more important, and the ends of a greater good DO justify the means, particularly and perhaps only in this case. We live in extraordinary times and time is ticking down rapidly.

We must be willing to break the entire system, tear down the institutions and replace everything with a more ecological and less humane substitute. Many will call my philosophy 'eco-terrorism' or 'environmental extremism', and yet I only condone violence to prevent the environmental massacres that continue unhindered and only if things do not unfold the way they must and probably will. If we can't fix this peacefully, we have to be prepared to fight for our lives, quite literally. We should slowly ramp up civil dissent with clear environmental demands. We should target the practices and institutions who wilfully ruin the world. We should go to the streets again and again and again in bigger and bigger numbers, with bigger and bigger plans. The threat of terrible action will force investors to retreat so we might be saved from extreme lengths.

But eventually this has to coalesce around elections and politics. We need people to engage with politics like never before and to decide somehow to all support one party. Maybe this party could be the extreme greens, or the 'life' party, or the 'one purpose, one party' party, but we need to somehow unite our disparate needs and desires into one inarguable goal or set of goals. We should have a national 50-year-plan at least. Left and Right are meaningless in the face of environmental catastrophe. Just vote Green, please. Eamon is the nicest chap in Ireland. They're no longer a 'single-issue' party. They are the 'only-issue' party.

I just want to quickly also point out that in Ireland's case of Proportional Representation democracy, all you need to do is field thousands and thousands of candidates to win more seats. One very stupid party had nearly enough votes, but not enough candidates to win the last election. They're very stupid for lots of reasons, but this is their latest in a long line of fumbling. The idea that a lovely swing to the Left will save us from the sad retreat to the Right we've seen in recent years is dreaming in fairy land. Look around the world. Many people seem to recognise the cold hard maths of survival and sustainability, but they're afraid to vote for a 'single-issue' party like the Greens. They will not vote for what they think is a fantasy either, whether that's starry-eyed socialist idealists on the left, or the hairy tree-huggers on the far left. We need to make the Green issue very real for people, and we need to bring it to the centre and to the right. Environmentalism is not about loveliness and fraternity; it is about survival and economics.

Reasonable people need to take up the cause in large numbers. If enough people knock on your door asking you to vote green you surely will, even if you don't know any better. Children and teenagers have immense power in this regard. If squads of young sweet kids could organize themselves, they could melt hearts on doorsteps and take control of democracy. Young people these days mostly don't read though, so it's up to you to tell them how much power they have over their futures. Next election I hope to see legions of children out knocking on doors. They need to get tuned in; they are the ones who will suffer most.

People of yesteryear had the unity of religion to make their efforts have meaning in the grander scheme of things. We lack that now in our daily lives, but I would never advocate a return to the superstition and misguided teachings of the churches and temples. Instead we must develop a new spiritual and fundamental purpose to our lives based on the reality our environment presents us with. Our achievements need to be measured in their environmental impacts instead of their financial ends or the immeasurable impact on our happiness. We need to value human life against the life of all living things. What have you planted? What have you grown? What have you nurtured in nature? And gosh don't talk to me about your children; a dog can have children. But a dog can't grow its own food. Which is a higher indicator of intelligence?

It's almost impossible to imagine any wide scale uptake of any given ideology or set of beliefs, so it is going to be vanishingly difficult to ever satisfactorily achieve the full support necessary to do what needs to be done. It is the dreadful responsibility of anyone who has enough intelligence and awareness to pursue all ends to achieve the survival of our species and our way of life into the far future, however painful and lonely that may be. It may well be that it will fall to small groups and cells around the world to attempt large scale changes through collective action and persuasion. But for anyone willing to take up this fight, there can be no nobler cause, or more meaningful expenditure of this finite life than in the pursuit of the goal of sustainability and survival.

There will necessarily be soldiers in this fight who will sacrifice everything for this cause, as every noble cause has ever cost the blood of its martyrs. It seems dramatic in this secular time to talk of martyrs, but sacrifice for the greater good is a universal human trait, and this cause will demand blood. We must be prepared to give it, peacefully at

first, but then painfully if needs be. The further I describe
what I feel will inevitably come to pass, the more I feel
resigned to a horrible less than optimum outcome in any of
the domains I have described previously. There will come a
time in this lifetime when conflicts and huge human suffering
will occur and we will resolutely have to stand back and say;
better them than us. There may come a time when nations will
need to wilfully inflict harm on other nations in order to serve
the greater good. Good intentions may lead us into hell, but
hopefully back out again.

I normally detest any tribal sense of
nationalism, but in the case of Ireland and nations like her,
there are no more natural unit of focus to bring about change
than the national institutions already in place and the island
itself. We must unite our nations to face the coming battles
and conflicts and efforts. We must have a war-time mentality
to our dedicated cause. Therefore, it will be imperative in the
future, I feel, to instil a deep nationalism and patriotism
behind clear national goals; goals we haven't got yet. We must
in Ireland replace republicanism and unionism with
environmentalism. I fear this will be necessary as a means of
defence as well as attack. Other nations will break, and suffer
great stresses that potentially we could avoid, and we cannot
save everyone on our lifeboat island. I absolutely abhor any
trace of racism and expression of pure ethnicity, but we will
have to close our borders in the future and we will have to be
united and strong behind our walls to weather some of the
coming storms, so we must do away with our sense of ethnic
and spiritual difference. The only differences between us are
falsehoods espoused by fools. We should be one island.
Whole. For environmental reasons and nothing else. The
people of the North are either badly represented or not
represented at all in Westminster. We can promise a much
better share under a green banner that has nothing at all to do
with Eire.

We are all one species, with one responsibility,

and it doesn't matter where you came from, or what you've suffered. You still have to make a positive net contribution to this world and that can really only be done through collective effort and purpose, best encapsulated by national pride and sovereignty of borders. We must take a stand as a nation and stop simply following in the footsteps of our 'betters'. The very best vehicle for change on a global scale is pressure on a national scale everywhere it can be mustered. There is not yet the suitable international governance mechanisms in place, though of course one day there shall have to be.

I suggest the government could help enforce unity by adding a new institution to the world. Why don't we assign every indivual in the nation a 'unit' of community; a list of a 50 or so random people who are now their 'unit'. These units fall somewhere between a family and a tribe/community. Instead of the government or the big bad world being responsible for the suffering or wellbeing of people, we should make it the responsibility of these units. If someone is suffering unfairness, indignity and injustice in your unit, then you're at fault until you have done everything that is in the power of your unit to do to improve that individual's lot. These units could be allocated resources and their contributions could be measured and tested. Family units and community units have been around since the dawn of time, but we've never really organized them officially to serve the duty we know they serve anyway. It should take a village to raise a child, even if that village is inside a metropolis. This is just a small step among many giant leaps we have the potential to make.

There are also things globally that surely must come to pass if we are to have a decent future. Again, I unfortunately have to condone a certain level of cold hard cruelty when we look at the big picture. There is an ugly truth in proposing population controls. There will have to be mechanisms in place for the control of populations in certain places and due to certain conditions especially. There's no point millions of babies being born in a refugee camp, or in a warzone. It's just a sad waste of human life, and our precious resources. Equally, when we know a life will be unviable for anything but a short life and we can stop it early enough, then we should. This is only morally acceptable due to the climate crisis. It would be nearly intolerable otherwise. If you are destined to die before 5 then it is extremely unlikely you will make anything but a heavier carbon footprint. I know that is cruel and beyond contemplation; it's just the truth. Obviously the people are guilty of nothing and deserve better, but there is a cold hard truth of over-population. Why weigh yourself down with children when your suffering is already great and promises to be greater? And yet the controls will be automatically opposed by almost everyone on earth, to the point of violence. We will in the long term have to take up arms against those most ideologically opposed to the progress necessary for the survival of mankind, or those whose treatment of their subjects and citizens is so intolerable we cannot allow them to continue as if it were ok.

We all laugh at and direct our hatred towards North Korea, when just to the north, the second largest economy on earth is run in an even more brutal way, and we're all fine with doing business with them and allowing their people to travel freely around the free world. It's ludicrous. Free citizens of the world are not afforded even a shred of privacy and freedom when they visit these medieval backwaters that have traded their way to ill-gotten wealth like the Saudis or Chinese. It is intolerable to be allowed to continue and no matter what conflict it causes; we must make global pariahs of these monsters until they collapse. We will then have to wade in and fix them, or let them fight and starve. Better them than us. And yet China foresaw the need for population control a generation ago. They will be the very last ones we ask to do it again, because despite whatever evil China might do on a regular basis, they have potentially expanded the life of humanity by many decades by paying a price in human life for decades. We actually all owe China an enormous debt and the only way to pay it is to follow suit and elect to have a one-child policy and a worldwide commitment by multitudes to simply forgo parenthood.

There just **needs** to be a one-child policy imposed upon the world, voluntarily if at all possible, but any way at all in the long run. Obviously I want us all to choose to not have children at all so that there will be so much more literal 'lebensraum' for all our children. I am a teacher and I consider all children to be my children. Every interaction that every person has with every child shapes that child's future and world view. Everyone has parental responsibility in an emergency. In Plato's Republic, he advocated the collective rearing of children. It really does take a village to raise a child. We don't all need to have our own. The simplest and easiest method of saving the world from the hubris and short-sightedness of humanity is to shrink the population enormously. I know the problem of how you look after the old people is a major issue, but I for one am more than willing to sacrifice my miserable drug-flavoured death for a future in which YOUR children, and Mohammed's children, and Xin's children, and Mark's, can just HAVE a future. If we can't do this, then we have to look at uglier solutions.

Eventually I can even foresee an outright resource grab with force becoming justified in someone's mind within just a lifetime, because even if you are from a nice peaceful law-abiding place, there will be lots of dangerous groups and warlords who will seek to upset the balance. And remember that China will always have its *casus belli* due to its sacrifice. Other ruthless people like me will rise up in places, with the far right, the far left and everywhere else, and they will destabilise and topple countries, start conflicts and grab resources themselves. If you know that your neighbouring country is descending into anarchy, and that key resources must be carefully managed even if the people are suffering from the lack of their exploitation, you may see it as imperative that responsible control is achieved.

In fact, I would advocate certain resources being forcefully confiscated immediately and preserved from humanity completely, such as swathes of the Amazon or Indonesia or the Congo. By whom, I'm not sure; I'm the only one I trust. I would advocate the immediate and violent establishment of a global fishing ban, enforced with extreme prejudice, for the good of the oceans, what little hope is left for them. I'd do it myself if I could. Once again, human lives mean nothing to me when compared to the wealth and diversity of all the life those humans endanger. We must adopt this attitude. Anything else is suicide. Niceness is about to get us all killed.

There are cities that need to be razed to the ground, production facilities that should be buried and generators that need to be destroyed, whether the people who depend on them agree or not, and I would eventually condone extreme action such as the destruction of such evil facilities, the boycott and utter seclusion of their employees, and scuppering and obstruction of all efforts. People who burn coal for a living should be looked down upon like hangmen or fools. We should be even prepared to destroy property ourselves. No one who stands purely for this cause should ever suffer the heavy hand of a justice system built on whispers and lies. The truths about this world, morality, and what's right and wrong, are not derived from god, but by close observation of the truth of our lives and proved by trial and experiment. It is not good enough to expect patience now, as these gigantic super-tankers that are our societies turn on a dime and completely reconfigure every aspect of our daily lives. We need to break it and remake it. There is no other real viable way of making our civilisation resistant to the ravages of time.

I call for the revolution to begin soon. We don't

have much time. But it's not all doom and gloom! There is lots of reason for great optimism about the human capacity to overcome adversity, and lots of reason to be excited about the potential our future holds. I have pointed out the seemingly obviously almost-divine purpose that lays before us on a cosmic scale with regards to space exploration and colonisation, but I cannot impress upon you how thrilling an opportunity is within the grasp of our short lifetime. There are plans afoot to go here, there and everywhere. We definitely want to have a human presence on the moon and Mars, but I feel there is an often overlooked intermediate that we should be directing all of our energy and resources towards. We should build space stations! What wouldn't I give, burn or sacrifice to see a living zoo out among the stars? We can have cities and nations in orbit if we want to.

There is no limit to the size and scope of the projects we might be able to achieve simply in orbit around earth. We are in the early stages of the development of asteroid capture and resource harvesting from space directly. The person, company or country who can capture the first big ice chunk out there and bring it to earth to be an orbiting gas station is going to earn trillions. There could be diamonds the size of cars whizzing around up there, not that diamonds have any value whatsoever; it would just be cool to capture one. I want to see us live the sci-fi dreams of the post-Apollo era. I can't understand how we've settled for anything less than absolute Jetsons or Star Trek levels of advancement in space exploration.

Ireland is a small country; we explore space with the EU, but we should dream enormously for our own ambitions too. We have the potential to create national projects of global worth. We have vast areas of sea and ocean and air space under our protection in between the two richest continents on earth. We should take a stand about who can use it and how, no matter the economic cost. It was a disgusting disgrace to allow American war planes to use Shannon, but we do worse things with our ocean jurisdiction. We allow super-trawlers and ruthless fishermen to strip them clean. We allow dirty and blatantly unsustainable gas and oil exploitation happen in our waters, by people who don't live in our country or care about our environment. We build off-shore wind turbines that we know are actually contributing more C02 than simply burning the bloody fossil fuel, due to their maintenance and construction. It's absurd that we are so quick to think there will be magical solutions that actually require us to INCREASE our industrial capacity.

Be utterly wary of any supposed environmentalist who proposes that we can all profit greatly by building a green future. That is a dirty pernicious lie and it is damaging our society irreversibly at the moment. It is definitively what I call painting the future in rainbows. It is the last ditch effort of the oil industry to remain on top. There will be an enormous cost in lives and labour and resources to save the earth. And potentially only a few of us will remain wealthy and able enough to truly enjoy it in all its splendour. Even if we have to reduce our population down to a bare minimum to save the world, at least someone will be there to see the future of this magical globe. We must set out on a path of dramatic change. We must dream big.

I see one of two potential futures coming true. One; we will spiral out of control and collapse globally in an irredeemable way as we fight bit by bit to preserve the world in the face of the onslaught of inexorably mounting human consumption, or two; we will reduce our population by at least half in one lifetime and only grow beyond that in space, reverse our habitat destruction and barely limit our global warming to a tolerable level with hugely imaginative and futuristic yet-to-be-invented solutions. Which of these two do you think most likely?

Finally, in terms of the likelihood of our imminent destruction in one lifetime or two, I will now offer a list of odds on the things I think are most likely to make this world intolerable fairly soon:

Global irreversible famine due to lack of fertilisers and petro-chemical industry 2-1

Deoxygenated ocean leading to famine 3-1

Famine caused by pollinator extinction 3-1

Some kind of global famine in the next thirty-odd years 11-10

Collapse of major nation due to land loss 11-10

Global apocalyptic war in 100 years 10-1

Radiation contamination destroying world's society in 100 years 10-1

Absolute collapse within 100 years 2-1

Absolute collapse within 200 years odds-on favourite 9-10

Taking bets here folks. If you want to offset carbon and don't believe you're ruining the world, you could make some money.

So, the end is nigh, and we must act in the most dramatic and revolutionary way that humans have ever reacted to anything, and we must do it immediately. We who are young enough to fear it will live to see the end of the kind of world that has been taken for granted for two or more generations. One way or another, our lives will be changed beyond all recognition. We have a choice to make between sitting back, or how we best decide to intervene. Changes will come to our lives; to the food that we eat, to the bedding and clothing we use, to the transport systems and infrastructure we have come to rely on, to the way we interact with other humans and cultures, and to how we live every single other aspect of our lives. Embrace it or be overcome.

My next book will probably be about Justice and legal systems around the world, and how punishment and rehabilitation are treated and analyse what outcomes seem to be most successful. I mention this here because it is yet another institution where environmental change should be felt massively. It is so stupendously wasteful to lock people up and provide for their needs with huge labour and resource costs while we neither really punish nor really rehabilitate the worst and most egregious offenders. Every single institution, organization and endeavor of any kind needs to immediately pause and rethink how it will look in the dawn of sustainability. Prisoners at the very least should be able to grow their own food and produce their own resources, you would think.

Every single thing needs to change. Every single thing needs to be reinvested. No institution on Earth will stand in its current shape for very long without being made to look foolish. Take the catholic church for example. Never before has any organization looked so perversely fallible and yet they cling fiercely to the wealth and privilege and 'infallibility' they possess despite its flagrant contradiction of its own teaching and values. Remember the eye of the needle and the rich man. Maybe priests should use their resources and facilities to help people rather than reap a tithe. How many empty bedrooms are there in parochial houses around the world? Tens of thousands. While homelessness exists. The shame of having been baptized by these charlatans hangs heavily over my head. It is just one of millions of institutions. We must change everything to change the future.

We have entered into a period of human development where any number of wildly unbelievable futures could all very well come to pass, and the most likely seem to be the worst. Who knows what kinds of governments and nations there will be a hundred years from now. There's never been a world map you could hardly keep from one year to the next throughout human history, and the coming decades promise to be some of the most tumultuous in human history following the great peace of the west for the past few decades. It will be a rude and rough awakening for millions of young people, who will emerge into the light one day, angry, and full of resentment for all the minutes we let tick by while the world was literally burning around us. The youth will rise, and you'll learn that Greta was being nice. Nothing will stay the same. You can either hold on and hope not to be trampled and gored, or aptly grab the bull by the proverbials.

There is more I could I have written in this book. I could have expanded on and told the story of a number of other ocean-wide contaminations, though that section was long already, or I could have focussed in on the details of the many environmental disasters and spills that have occurred throughout history. I could have told a great many extinction stories. I could have explored exactly all the limits of all the various minerals we need; everything is finite. I didn't write about many of the widespread effects the hormones in our meat and dairy are having. I didn't talk about the absurd obesity, inactivity and diabetes running through the population like wildfire. I didn't talk about the space debris we're quickly accumulating in orbit that might prevent our future expansion and dependence on communications technology. I didn't describe how many hectares of land are burning worldwide at all times. I could go on. The reason I won't go on is it never ends. There is only one real problem, and that problem is obviously us. Humanity. A plague of hominid-shaped locusts.

I don't know what else I can do. I have gathered here overwhelming evidence that humanity is about to bring about its own collapse and destruction due to its current paradigm. If the evidence is not enough to convince people that we need to take drastic action, then all we can do is appeal to a higher power. Perhaps someone will write a new gospel, so that people who simply need their spiritual vacuum filled can be harnessed to what needs to be done. I feel desperate now as I come to the end of this book that I might fail to put in that one silver bullet sentence that is really going to convince you to go out and change the world around you immediately. The spuds you plant will be the best you ever taste! Letting trees grow and die naturally is the only way to capture carbon! You can't eat meat every day! Recycle! We need Zeus or Odin or Brahmin or someone to descend from the heavens and give us all a collective slap upside the head and wake us up. There is a challenge laid out in front of us of cosmic consequence that is obvious and open to all in the preservation and promotion of life off this one little rock in the screaming maelstrom of the universe. The universe is our oyster if we can just make it so.

And can we please all be a bit nicer to each other too? Is that too much to ask? Let me please leave you with some ideas for how to live your life. It's not my place to give commandments. Let these be more like guidelines.

1: Read (no good telling you, but tell others)

2: That which is right and good is that which has the greatest and longest lasting improvement in wellbeing for yourself and your environment. (Read Sam Harris; The Moral Landscape)

3: Question everything. Challenge your own beliefs on a daily basis.

4: Do unto others what you would have them do unto you.

5: Reproduction is a privilege and not a right.

6: Everyone's child is your child

7: Stop lying about hallucinations and self-delusions. You didn't see a real ghost or an alien or a saint or god, however much you believe it. We've all hallucinated; some of us know it.

8: Read. It's a shame we've almost made it taboo to be a reader. Certainly young people think you're automatically a fool if you read. It's a disgrace. I teach these kids every day. Their parents should be gelded for their illiteracy. I make no bones about it.

9: Civility and politeness cost nothing but are worth everything.

10: Vote Green! In Ireland vote for Eamon or whoever your local, obviously inferior, equivalent is. Eamon is even handsome. Got it all, our Eamon.

11: Oh and stop burning shit.

I'm sorry it's all so grim; it's just the way it had to be. Please spread this message far and wide. I'm also sorry I have to charge you money to read this, but I NEED the money. I will buy land and plant forests with every euro I can muster. I will run for election. If you can spend your money on your own forests and political campaigns, then brilliant! If not, send me more money. I'll name a tree after you.

In this book there is fear, but there is also hope. It may seem that I have tried too hard to focus on fear and have left little room for hope, but please, if you knew me and saw me speak about the future I hope we have, you would know I am a well-spring of hope. Part of my philosophy is that fear and hope are opposites and without one there cannot be the other. In my opinion it is only worth fearing that for which you hope for a better outcome. There is no point in fearing death because there is no hope of you living forever. I outline fear to stir hope. Please don't throw away your life on hopelessness. We cannot afford to lose you. If you know as I know that there is a way open to us, we need you. You have become an exceptionally valuable creature in a seemingly inter-galactic level of responsibility. I feel alive for the first time. We must not let each other down now, not after all that has been done to bring us here. I have decried the evils of the human world but there is also beauty, ingenuity and the sisterhood of man. We are truly wonderful specimens to behold.

PS… S.W.A.L.K (ask grandma; it's sweet) and BTW, on the day I finished, the population had reached 7.784 billion. More than 40 million more people now grace the world in the time it took me to pour this paltry book out. Hooray! Go team. Well done everyone. Can we please stop now?

And please do read the other last bit too. It's important.

7: References: For you

I have struggled with how to present this. I advocate an active audience who takes ownership of their own understanding, and it is perhaps not the best guide to new researchers to lay out hundreds of separate documents, where one figure comes from one, its assessment from another, and another number from a third. If this were a thesis I would simply include the exact evidence to support my idea and exclude that which doesn't. Academics are not saints. This isn't a thesis; it is a plea and prophecy of doom. Rather than print ten pages to prove myself right despite whatever contrary evidence there is, I will instead make a bibliography website where you can explore my deductions. Below you will find both sides of the fishing industry's numbers and both sides of the oil fiasco and in gapfiner.org you can see every side of the population question. Instead of a bibliography of my sources, I will list what I think are the BEST resources; the most concise and convincing documents and sources I have come across. I bring you all the leading authorities of the world; see what they have to say. There is so much more, but in a world where people think 'the science isn't settled', what a waste of time to spell it out for those few of you who actually care enough to read the references. If you are here, you already care enough. You probably already know a lot, but the half-life of facts and the stupendous scientific advancement of modernity is impossible to keep up with. I will also include pieces that aren't expressly in the book, but form parts of its thinking, or were on the shortlist. Consider this a list of recommendations for you to pursue later, in preparation for the great fight to come. At least look at these URLs. The titles alone should chill you to the core. Our only salvation is in people finding these things out for themselves. Enjoy.

Ocean pollution and water type stuff

noaa.gov/education/resource-collections/ocean-coasts/ocean-pollution

ourworldindata.org/plastic-pollution

worldwildlife.org/magazine/issues/fall-2019/articles/plastic-in-the-ocean

woi.economist.com/one-ocean-one-response-addressing-plastic-pollution/

itopf.org/knowledge-resources/data-statistics/statistics/

blog.resourcewatch.org/2019/02/07/there-were-137-oil-spills-in-the-us-in-2018-see-where-they-happened/

response.restoration.noaa.gov/oil-and-chemical-spills/oil-spills/largest-oil-spills-affecting-us-waters-1969.html

unesco.org/new/en/natural-sciences/ioc-oceans/focus-areas/rio-20-ocean/blueprint-for-the-future-we-want/marine-pollution/facts-and-figures-on-marine-pollution/

nrdc.org/stories/ocean-pollution-dirty-facts

unesco.org/new/en/natural-sciences/ioc-oceans/focus-areas/rio-20-ocean/blueprint-for-the-future-we-want/ocean-acidification/facts-and-figures-on-ocean-acidification/

nca2014.globalchange.gov/report/our-changing-climate/ocean-acidification data.oecd.org/water/waste-water-treatment.htm

unstats.uhttps://unesdoc.unesco.org/ark:/48223/pf00002475
53n.org/unsd/environment/wastewater.htm

Extinction

nationalgeographic.com/environment/2019/04/ocean-
species-disappear-faster-climate-change-impacts-cold-
blooded-animals-harder/

onegreenplanet.org/environment/marine-species-extinction-
and-plastic-pollution/

sciencealert.com/we-now-know-what-killed-the-sea-life-in-
the-world-s-deadliest-mass-extinction   (spoiler; it's us)

wwf.panda.org/our_work/biodiversity/biodiversity/

biologicaldiversity.org/programs/biodiversity/elements_of_
biodiversity/extinction_crisis/

un.org/sustainabledevelopment/blog/2019/05/nature-
decline-unprecedented-report/

Resource scarcity

datatopics.worldbank.org/consumption/

yearbook.enerdata.net/total-energy/world-consumption-
statistics.html

bp.com/en/global/corporate/energy-economics/statistical-
review-of-world-energy.html

iea.org/data-and-statistics/charts/world-total-final-
consumption-by-region-1971-2017

ourworldindata.org/fossil-fuels

wrforum.org/publications-2/publications/

usgs.gov/centers/nmic/historical-global-statistics-mineral-and-material-commodities

un.org/esa/esa99dp5.pdf

fao.org/state-of-fisheries-aquaculture

gov.uk/government/news/fishing-industry-in-2018-statistics-published

ec.europa.eu/fisheries/facts_figures_en

ibisworld.com/united-kingdom/market-research-reports/marine-fishing-industry/

globalfishingwatch.org

iss-foundation.org

Global warming and sea level rise

climate.nasa.gov/evidence/

ncdc.noaa.gov/global-warming

skepticalscience.com/global-warming-scientific-consensus.htm

conservation.org/stories/11-climate-change-facts-you-need-to-know un.org/en/sections/issues-depth/climate-change/

carbonbrief.org/analysis-why-scientists-think-100-of-global-warming-is-due-to-humans

co2.earth/global-warming-update

oceanservice.noaa.gov/facts/sealevel.html

climate.nasa.gov/vital-signs/sea-level/

www.nationalgeographic.com/environment/global-warming/sea-level-rise/

ocean.si.edu/through-time/ancient-seas/sea-level-rise

nca2014.globalchange.gov/report/our-changing-climate/sea-level-rise

Other. Go find more. Attach 'scholarly article' behind your searches on google if you've got the chops.

gapfinder.org for amazing representations of population.

The New Scientist magazine and other scientific publications. Journalism will never cover the truth of our development like the scientific journals. Pollution doesn't sell newspapers. It barely sells scientific journals.

Vice news documentaries on the environment.
Richard Dawkins and Christopher Hitchens on god.
Sam Harris on morality. Almost nowhere else is correct.

Read the Bible, the Torah and the Quran. Read the eastern tripe too. Not enough of you have actually read these books as simply books. They are allegorical drivel from another millennium. Great books though.

Most importantly of all: A deep sense of scepticism and distrust of everything and everyone. I have found that if you approach life with the attitude that if there is something that everyone thinks and believes then it is probably wrong, then you will be a happier person. Always question every given principle. Always ask where is the evidence and justification to back stuff up. I am currently reading and investigating about the pros and cons of cannibalism, not that I have a hankering, but simply because I assume everyone thinks it's wrong and horrific, so I bet there's some profound reason why for SOMEONE SOMEWHERE it won't be. And it turns out some people eat their placenta. It's really very good for you. You live and learn; I'd presumed you'd get rabies or something. Always assume everyone is wrong, including yourself. You'll enjoy more pleasant surprises than unpleasant ones.

Go forth and stop multiplying.

Get informed. Get angry. Get organised.

I'm gonna smoke a phat wun.